The 5 Commandments of Self-Love

A Journey to Honoring & Accepting Yourself

Tiffany A. Wright, MSW

ISBN: 978-1-0878-5471-7

This is dedicated to the ancestors who through both love and pain, taught me the value of acceptance and unapologetic authenticity. To mommy and papa.

"I exist as I am and that is enough."

— Walt Whitman

Table of Contents

Preface

Getting to the place of exploring the impact and stains of my childhood and adult traumas sparked an interest within me to explore my motivations, narratives, and understanding of my place in the world. I learned to be open to receiving insight into myself, the world, and the interconnectedness of the two. I began to see that so much of me was attached to people and experiences outside of myself. It was my insecurity, fear, and doubt that fueled a lot of my decisions and relationships. The more self-aware I became, the more I realized that I could massively improve on my boundary setting, expressing myself in a vulnerable and sensitive way, and in my self-care practice. Of most importance was being able to understand my interpersonal skills. Interpersonal refers to all the ways that we relate to, interact with and communicate with others. In my introspection, I came to the understanding that a central focus of my personal development needs to be self-love.

The journey thus far has been uncomfortable and painful at times and filled with freedom and ease at other times.

Unless one is raised with exposure to an understanding of self-love, the concept, like any alternate or foreign lifestyle, must grow on you intermittingly. I've come to understand that committing to self-love is a lifestyle. Certain types of choices characterize it. They are choices that involve harmony between choosing what's best you while honoring others as well. It's about practicing gentleness, compassion, and grace for yourself, as well as for others. Self-love is most importantly, marked by persistent courage and unapologetic boldness.

Thus, knowing your truth, owning your truth, speaking your truth, and walking in your truth while contributing to the world, is surely a cornerstone of the foundation of a self-love centered life.

This book is a bit of a personal memoir of lessons I've learned from my personal journey, as well as insights collected in observation of other people's lives that I know personally and have come across in my work in the mental health field. In no way do I believe that the words that you will read are absolute truth; however, I do believe that it's possible to obtain insightful questions to ask yourself as you spend intentional time strengthening self-love and cultivating personal growth. I hope that you take what may serve and leave what you may not. The topic of self-love is something that I'm very passionate about, and I believe it to be tied to my purpose of healing.

Introduction

To begin exploring what self-love is, I think it would serve us to begin with the foundational word; love. Love is a concept that seems simple in theory yet complex in lived experience. It is a subjective notion of how one feels about or relates to a person, experience, or location. We use the term love about people that we have close relationships with, those we don't know and even those we admire from afar. We use it to describe our appreciation or attachment to items we desire or have in our lives. We use it to describe our affinity of a feeling. Furthermore, while some use it as merely a term of endearment, others use it to describe their commitment and loyalty to a person, people, community or cause. Thus, there is no absolute definition of what love is, whether as a verb or a noun. Consequently, if there's no true definition of love in relation to an external existence, there is surely much variability in the internal interpretation of the word.

How do we come to learn and understand what love means? Where and how do we grasp its complexity? Just like most of our narratives of the world, we come to understand what love means thru interaction and knowledge passed down to us from adults around us.

Adults explain it to us in different ways as children that certain actions define love; that certain relationships are defined by love. The true complexity is not that maybe our caretakers explain what love is, but we observe our surroundings, both in and out of our homes, and come to make associations of what love looks like.

We take these explanations to heart. They shape our understanding of the world. They shape our understanding of ourselves. The drawback of learning about love this way is that it comes with human limitations. The explanation and modeling of healthy love may be very limited. What someone defines as love can be very limiting. Likewise, what someone else defines as love can offer an expansive insight into its possibilities. Regardless, love or ideas of love are heavily influenced by our caretakers, by our teachers, by our spiritual advisers, and then, of course by the media. We are born with an intuitive sense of knowing what serves us and what doesn't, but due to the stages of human development and the development of the critical brain, the ability to consciously be aware of our intuition does not develop until adulthood. Children often have a stable sense of security, which makes them see the best in others. They are often open to people, and assume everyone "loves" them. Unless a child grows up in an environment that is marked by abuse or neglect, it takes time to learn the complexity of humans. It is life's lessons, coupled with the development of critical thinking skills, in which children grow into adolescents and adults, then begin to challenge what love looks like and does not look like.

We must ask ourselves – As children, what models of love were we often exposed to? We witness love from different sources, or maybe the presence of love isn't truly experienced. As a child, one may recognize the love of a caretaker with a child, love between siblings, or love between extended family members. For most people, the models of love may come from traditional family arrangements. However, there are growing numbers of untraditional families or environments in which children are challenged to understand love. The growing number of blended families breeds circumstances where children learn that people that are not their biological parents, can love them fully. Some children grow up being hospitalized and see the care their medical staffs provide as "love." Children maneuvering foster care are often faced with testing their caregivers (foster parents) and not often feeling loved because of the complexity of their relationship. How does one who feels they've been "given up" by or taken away from their biological parent understand love? Children who grow up institutionalized or even experience life in boarding schools are often separated from anyone that may love them. Let's consider, as children, how did we experience love? Was it gentle, compassionate and supportive? Or was it abusive, controlling and removed? What about children whose complete reference of love comes thru observing others?

As a child, I remember that the most pensive vision of love came thru my favorite films and music. Because my parents weren't together, and I didn't have a model of love between two people to witness in my home daily, my outlook came from the skewed dramatization provided by none other than fairytales.

I think it's no surprise that most adults have a skewed sense of what love is because they didn't have a healthy model of love in their homes and/or they develop a romanticized understanding of love from the many stories of fantasies they've watched, read, or heard. More times than not, these fantasies were written to tap into the human imagination, provide entertainment, and a brief escape from reality – Stories that were considered pivotal in childhood. Media companies have taken stories that have been written centuries ago, reconfigured them, wrapped them up in a bow, and merchandised them to become central to the upbringing of children. The stories are turned into movies, TV shows, day-wear, pajamas, toys, and video games. How can one escape these stories?

Unlike most ideas that are created to tap into the imagination of children's stories about love, they are often not challenged by adults until a child becomes an adult, when another adult says "hey this is real life, it is not a fantasy." As children, you're told eventually that figures like the tooth fairy, Santa Claus or talking snowman, aren't real. These are a few of the many magical figures featured in childhood stories. Unfortunately, when it comes to love, that fantasy is held on by so many; consequently, because so much focus is put on romanticized love, the conversation of love outside of a fantastic contact is not really discussed.

Hence, when it comes to the fantastic idea or belief about love beyond the point of childhood, we graduate from mental or emotional referencing of fairytales that we read, to movies that we watch. Real-life is not the movies; there may be elements of how love stories can unfold, but for most of Hollywood's history, the depiction of love and relationships have been gravely misrepresented, overly romanticized, and incomplete to the complexities of humans and love.

In the movies, typical storylines consist of two heterosexual people who meet at random and fall in love at first sight. There are then the stories of people who meet serendipitously, and no matter what, life seems to bring them together consistently. Then we have the stories of people who found each other amid a hectic or traumatic experience or season in life. Now, of course, the storylines that are depicted in movies are totally passed possible because these circumstances may closely describe how you met your partner or someone you know. The problem is that most movies, especially pre-2005, didn't really and don't really get down to the nitty-gritty of how someone learns to love another, accept another, leave another, or choose to stay with someone because of reasons beyond love. Our movies leave our minds to fill in the gaps when in truthfully, it would be advantageous to explore the psychology of love. Now, of course, movies are for entertainment. Yet, not only are movies for entertainment, but they are also art, and art has the power to heal, educate, and empower. Hollywood is particular about how "true life" is depicted, but just think about the possibilities. What if our films stepped out of the box more to explore the psychology of love, as well as to highlight how self-love can affect one's ability to love?

I do believe there has been a storytelling evolution for both films and TV. Stories are grappling with the complexities of the human experience more. Within the last 15 years, filmmakers have improved in showing the versatility of how a personal journey of identity

8

exploration is becoming more important to people. With that, there are more scripts incorporating storylines of people embracing singleness, leaving unhealthy relationships, and choosing relationships that embrace the "humanity" of being in a relationship. I would attribute this shift to the impact of a generation more open to therapy, self-exploration, and prioritizing overall wellness. However, despite this evolution, the classic formula to romantic story still unfolds in many stories.

Let's examine some of these common themes, which often reflect helplessness, fragility, ego, and misguided action. We have the classic storyline of a man coming to "save" a woman but what we could address more is the reasoning as to why that woman feels that she needs saving, or why that man feels that he has to save that woman. We could even explore why a woman needs saving in the first place.

There are so many aspects of these idolized love narratives that are omitted. Audiences often experience limited insight into some of the psychological history, family upbringing, relationship history, or understanding of oneself that these movies and TV shows characters have experienced. We often see our characters meet in the present. From time to time, we have movies and shows that play on the power of the flashback. The flashback offers a glimpse into our character's psyche, but could always explore more. Scripts have progressed surely; because even think about the dominant image of our characters – Straight white people. These are not the only people to experience love, and thankfully, studios are finally rolling out more images that support that notion. There are fewer damsels in distress, fewer women "who need" to be in a relationship, there's more LGBTQ representatives, interracial and non-white couples. We see stories of more highlights of dating difficulties of current times.

What remains pervasive is the exclusion of understanding the depth of the human experience in need of healing. We don't see the deep pains and the requirements for growth.

There wasn't much struggle or challenge that couples had to face in romantic plotlines because there was always the hero that easily came to save the day. These characters were flat and underdeveloped. So much of their existence looked black and white and didn't really reflect the grey that is life. Princesses were either delicate and needy or strong, and warriors, but rarely was their exploration of the complexity behind such an identity. I could truthfully say that seeing one-dimensional women lead me to believe that 'who one is,' wasn't deeper than what others' could see. I didn't think that I would have to learn that my identity as a woman was deeper than that.

Just as one dimensional as the personalities and personas of these characters were, so was the love they experienced. It looked so simple; all you really had to do was see someone once or twice, have a brief conversation, and then you fall in love, get married, and live happily ever after. My goodness, what did they do to us?! The classic fairy tales in no way personified what the development of a romantic relationship looked like.

Indeed, with such a dense and oversimplified idea of romantic or platonic love, it is no surprise that most children grow into adults with a disconnection from what love can be. Love is seen as an experience of fantasy and ease. We take this idea into all of our relationships, and when the experiences we have with others don't align with the ideals, it is according to this unrealistic reference that we categorize our relationships as un-loving or undesirable. There is a high possibility that we do often indulge in unhealthy and un-loving relationships; however, at the same time, it is important that we understand the complexities of love and the depth of its dimensions.

An aspect of love's complexities that we may not see is the immense amount of compassion, patience, acceptance, and openness that encompasses a healthy and safe love experience. Sure, we see the dramas consisting of betrayal and broken hearts, but those are often the side effects of relationships lacking the previous mention. We don't see the intense work it may take for someone to be in a relationship because of their experiences, how it takes constant self- awareness, and forgiveness. Love is not something that "just" happens. It is an experience that we choose to open ourselves to have. However, if we see and understand love to be random, spontaneous and something that people "fall" into, then we don't realize the agency that truly exists in relationships. We have the agency to choose how we show up for others and our relationships. We have agency to choose how we treat others. Nothing "just happens." It helps us to understand why the awareness of ourselves and others is vital. This is why understanding self-love is important.

In the following text, we will explore how you have learned to understand love of self and others, in addition to challenging what you may need to unlearn in order to practice self-love. Extensive examples, personal vignettes, and psychological research will support our observation of the human experience connected to acceptance, healing, growth and self- actualization. We will explore self-love through the lens of five separate, yet intertwined commandments. The Five Commandments of Self Love are honor thyself, honor thy mind, honor thy body, honor thy spirit, and forgiveness of self and others. Throughout the book, you will see italicized questions. These are questions for you to ponder, process, and possibly journal about. May openness, transformation and the shift be with you.

The Journey to Understanding Self-Love

What Is Self-Love?

As children, perhaps we are granted with an older figure to tell us just to be ourselves; or let us know that we are unique. Perhaps, we have a person or people in our lives that affirm us. They tell us we are smart, capable, a winner, a hard worker, beautiful, strong, etc. These verbal affirmations are important because they contribute to our personal understanding of self-esteem. It is our uninhibited childhood boldness plus the words instilled to us by loved ones that allow us to live so courageously as children. We receive so many notions of love and encouragement outside of us that we often don't get to experience what internal love looks or feels like until we reach an age of self-awareness in our maturity, where or who we are, and how we relate to the world is a priority.

However, what if from a young age, we received verbal explanations of the different types of love? What if our learning and relating to love was not just about what we observed, but just like basic arithmetic, we were told love and self-love is "x."

Well, I imagine the world would be much different. I imagine people would be more compassionate. I imagine that people would be less judgmental. I imagine that people would be more open-minded and understand that because the concept of love is just as vast as the ocean, there is no one way to understand it, just as there is no one way to live life. *If I were to sit down with a child and introduce the concept of self-love, what would I say?*

At its very essence and most simplistic form, self-love is acceptance. Not partial acceptance, but full, whole, unapologetic, bold acceptance. Acceptance of your past and present. Acceptance of your choices. Acceptance of what occurred in your life, regardless if you consider it to be negative or positive. Acceptance for how you were born and the circumstances that you were raised. Acceptance of the opportunities you took advantage of and the opportunities that you missed. Acceptance of all the times you were accepted by others and acceptance of the times you were rejected. It's accepting every event, person or environmental stimuli that have shaped you into the person you are at this very moment.

Self-love is an act of embracing who you are, keeping in mind how you treat and look at yourself, as well as nurturing who you currently are, to become what you desire to be. Self-love is about self-awareness and personal acknowledgment. Most importantly, self-love is not a static concept. Just like love of others, love of self is and can be an ever-expanding concept for you to grasp. You will see love of self in different lights during different stages of your life. As you receive lessons on self-love, you will pass some life tests, be challenged by others, and down the line when you are presented with tests of self-love, you will have epiphanies, and realize those old ways of thinking and being, were not reflective of self-love and you will move forward with even higher elevated understandings.

Self-love encompasses many dimensions, and also how you love your outer and inner self. In its rawest form, it is the true representation of your self-image as well as your self-concept. Self-love is about your practices and how you truly honor yourself in the name of self-preservation and self-actualization. It has nothing to do with the pressures and expectations of anyone else. It has nothing to do with the show you put on for anyone. It has nothing to do with what you tell people about yourself. It has nothing to do with acts you do with or for others to satisfy your ego or get their approval. Our understanding of ourselves really begins from our experience in the womb.

There is a purity that exists in children in the first couple of years of life because they are essentially a clean slate. I say "essentially" because there is extensive research as to how the pre-natal experience shapes a growing fetus. Fetuses, infants, and toddlers may not be able to speak, but the brain registers their environmental stimuli. Our mammalian brain, which is the oldest area of our brains, responds to stimuli that threaten our survival like yelling (which is an indication of possible danger) or neglect. Infants exposed to any forms of abuse or neglect experience a shift in how their brains analyze safety. Exposure to environmental behaviors already begins to shape us before a sense of self-awareness develops. That coupled with the process of socialization, goes on to shape us.

We learn about ourselves thru our interactions with others, which is why our approval by others drives so much of what we do. According to Maslow's Hierarchy of Needs,[i] there is a five-tiered pyramid that describes what a human needs to reach self-actualization, the primary goal of life, achieving one's full potential, which are needs related to self-fulfillment. The tiers from bottom-up are *physiological needs* such as food, water, warmth and rest; *safety needs* such as the experience of security and safety, *belongingness and love needs* which are characterized by our intimate relationships and friends; *esteem needs* which relate to prestige and a feeling of accomplishment, and lastly, *self-actualization*.

The first two tiers, the physiological and safety needs, fall under our basic needs. As you can see, after our basic needs to survive are met, it is our sense of belonging and inclusion that follow. We are wired to need and thrive off connection to others. In addition to belonging is love. Looking at the following needs, there is no mention of self-love. Such a concept isn't included. Esteem for Maslow is defined by prestige and a feeling of accomplishment, which, if I can be honest, is often determined by others; others validation. We become prestigious because others have deemed us as so. More often than not, people feel a sense of accomplishment when others have awarded them, acknowledged their impact, or have provided positive re-enforcement of their efforts. This is what drives many of us.

We are often driven by the expectations of others. This is normal. It is the essence of socialization. As babies, children, and adolescents, we are given norms to follow. We are told to subscribe to religions without our say so. We are told the family rules. Parents even decide what activities you'll be involved in before you're of speaking age. We are put in schools, given clothes, food, and hairstyles without our input. We are told what behavior is acceptable. We are bombarded with images on phones, in books, in movies, and on TV that reinforces or present to us what is acceptable. When we act in a way approving of our caretakers, teachers, spiritual leaders, etc. we are told we are good. When we step out of those boundaries, we are told that we are being bad or are a disappointment. We are unknowingly pressured to live up to rigid expectations without any concern of how we may want to actually live our lives.

For a developing brain, a child is looking to understand the world and themselves. How children receive this knowledge is provided by reinforcement. Thus, a positive affirmation, a smile, a gift, a display of affection, or receiving a positive grade, are all ways that we provide positive reinforcement to children. As children grow, the reinforcement isn't just about what is explicitly being said; it is also about the unmentioned. Implicit communication, such as body language can be just as impactful as a direct compliment. As a child, we navigate our world intuitively and honestly. We are often inquisitive, ask questions, and speak our minds with little filtering. The older we get we learn to determine social cues of appropriateness, decorum, and etiquette. These filters begin to impede on our connection to our intuition. Children, especially up until the age of about 8, are very intuitive and can respond to people purely based on energy. This is why a baby can begin crying instantly when one stranger holds them and smiles when another holds them.

Around the age of 10/11, when a pre-adolescent enters puberty and the developmental phase of their conscious identity formation has begun, all their collective experiences up to that point have impacted their sense of self-love. According to developmental psychologist, Jean Piaget, age 12 is when youth begin to develop what is known as theoretical, counterfactual and hypothetical thinking. They can think about possibilities of outcomes, and focus on probability. With this progress in cognitive development, comes the process of pulling together the cumulative experiences and knowledge that a young person has been exposed to. If during their development, there has been a limited or no modeling of self -love, self-care, or positive esteem, these concepts do not intercede in one's understanding of abstract ideas that shape their lived experience.

The child then becomes the adult who has a distant relationship with the abstract concept of self-love. Self-love becomes a concept one first needs to grasp, and then something that one needs to learn how to live. If you are not taught and shaped by an understanding of self-love, it truly has to become a part of your lifestyle, and what matters most is that you understand that self-love is a lifestyle. It's about the small steps you take every day to ensure that you are honoring yourself. It is not a destination. There is always something to unpack. There is always a way to love yourself deeper. There is no point in your life where there is no more room for learning. The more we learn about ourselves and about the world, the more we realize we don't know. When it comes to self-love, it really is about you learning who you are, how you perceive your value, and how you honor yourself. There are probably very few people in their senior age who not only truly know, understand, and accept themselves, but they have also come to accept their lives.

There are so many people who face the end of their life and begin to contemplate about the life they lived and reflect on decisions that bring about pride and regret. It's common that they think about how they didn't live their life to their full potential. In the book, "The Top 5 Regrets of Dying," author and palliative care nurse, Bonnie Ware, recorded the reflections and most pensive regrets of some of her patients over the course of the last 12 weeks of their life and expanded on them in her book. The top 5 regrets were as follows:

1. *"I wish I'd had the courage to live a life true to myself, not the life others expected of me."*
2. *"I wish I hadn't worked so hard."*
3. *"I wish I'd had the courage to express my feelings."*
4. *"I wish I had stayed in touch with my friends."*
5. *"I wish that I had let myself be happier."*

In further exploration of this last regret, she states, "This is a surprisingly common one. Many did not realize until the end that happiness is a choice. They had stayed stuck in old patterns and habits. The so-called 'comfort' of familiarity overflowed into their emotions, as well as their physical lives. Fear of change had them pretending to others and their selves that they were content when deep within, they longed to laugh properly and have silliness in their life again."[ii]

Consider from the above list, that these individuals and many others I'm sure who are preparing for transition thought about the relationships that they did not nurture. They reflect on the ways that others had a grave influence on how they decided to live their lives. They think about the ways that they did not live in their truth and seek out personal freedom. As you focus on your self-love journey, I challenge you to set an intention to not only be your best self but love yourself as best as you can and accept yourself. You will come to realize that no one has all the answers, and at the end of the day, we're living our lives the best way we can.

All in all, what you see from these regrets are people that didn't know how to love or honor themselves. You see, people that didn't permit themselves to embrace who they truly are. It could well be because the concept of self-love was distant or seemingly not obtainable for them. These reflections are far too common. Some believe that life isn't about experiencing joy or fulfillment or shouldn't be focused on the self at all. Often, those who are raised to prioritize community connection and family honor, as part of typical cultures defined by interdependence as opposed to independence, will evaluate their lives based on the lived experiences, and I believe that is beautiful. A doctrine of self-love can only be minimally applicable for individuals with those values, because in many ways, they may contradict.

However, it feels so much more powerful and impactful when our lives can be lived with intention. The intention to love ourselves as well as loving others. Because when we truly love ourselves, we open ourselves up to giving love to the world. The world needs love. It is love that heals. It is love that restores. It is love that is missing from the wounded, the confused, angered, the belittled, disenfranchised, and apathetic. If more of the world experienced love, it would be so many issues that could be eradicated.

I want you to know that self-love is not easy. I've said it many times and will continue to reiterate it throughout the book because it's an important truth that I've come to. Like with any practice, the more you do it, the more you walk in it, the more that it's the truth, the easier it becomes, and the more it fits you like a glove. See what happens before we really embark on a journey of intentionally learning to love ourselves; it's a psychological and spiritual adjustment. A great deal of self-awareness consists of getting in tune with the self. There's much to unlearn. There's much to learn, especially about yourself. There's much to learn when it comes to honoring yourself. As mentioned, walking in self-love takes courage because frequently, you present to some others, as a problem.

People have a problem when you have too much confidence or believe too much in yourself. People have a problem when you choose yourself over them. In self-love, there is a consistent practice of boundary setting. There are several types of boundaries: temporal, physical, sexual, intellectual, emotional, and material. People have a problem with hearing someone say no to them. People have a problem with people that they love creating boundaries between them. So because people, in general, have problems with self-love, it can be harder for an individual who sees the value in embarking on such a journey.

The Distant Concept That is Self-Love

If the psychological theory of attachment holds true, in regard to how we develop our identity and esteem, then it seems that self-love is distant as our awareness or models of self-love would be. Self-love would have to be something not only taught but observed. It would have to be learned. However, *is love something that is learned?* What we experience those first years with our caregivers is not love; it is attachment and reliability. We are looking for them to care for and nurture us, so in our efforts of respecting, being dependent on, and showing affection to them, we learn what it means to relate to and love others. *If a child develops their sense of safety and security in the world from their parents, then does that mean our sense of security can only be developed from external interactions?*

How our caregivers treat us, provides us with the core narratives of what to expect from others. In all of this, there seems to be something missing; the ability to see within ourselves the importance of respect and affection. We are taught to feel bad when we do something wrong. We are taught to forgive and share with others. We are taught to say nice things to others. Make or buy gifts for those you love. During holidays, as children, we petition to our parents to make cupcakes for the class. *There are so many opportunities in which we are instructed to please and honor others, but why are there rarely lessons about what we can do for ourselves? Is the notion of self-love natural or unnatural? Is the process of honoring one's self innate, or must it be learned?* The more years that pass, the more distant the concept of self-love seems to be. It becomes such a foreign idea, that once you hear the phrase, or begin to embark on such a journey, it requires adaptation.

It requires you to unlearn and release most behaviors, narratives, and thoughts that have come to define your way of living. Maybe you finally begin to realize how important it is to acknowledge, honor and accept who you are. We are encouraged to wear masks to be what our families, neighborhoods, and communities want or expect us to be. We are taught to consider others' comfort before our own. We are taught that those with voices, who speak up, and who say no are rebels or rude. We are told that too much truth is considered brash, so we learn how to be silent or finesse the way we express ourselves to others.

We are essentially taught how to make room for others while dishonoring ourselves. We become adults who don't want to or feel undeserving of taking up space in the world. It is in the silence, in the guilt, in the discomfort, and in the delusion, that we learn, our beings are of limited importance compared to the comfort of others. So much of our lives are driven by a mode of compromise that keeps us feeling that we live at the mercy of or are in obligation to other people and societal expectations. People live lifestyles, make choices, follow religions, get in marriages/relationships, have families and enter career fields because of disconnection from self and obligation.

An authentic lyric made popular by artist, designer, and entrepreneur Kanye West is, "everybody's insecure I'm just the first to admit." The reason that this statement is actually such a big deal and holds so much truth is that we are often driven by our insecurities. Our insecurities have the power to push us to prove something to someone, to seek validation by others, or actually create a barrier that prevents us from living a life that we would otherwise desire to live. Where Kanye West fell short in addressing the topic is actually asking, *why are we insecure? Or where does the insecurity stem from?* For you, the reader, I encourage you to raise these questions. It's really important as we are on our journey of discovery, growth, and love, which we ask ourselves questions like *Why do I do what I do? What motivates me? What puts forth a barrier and holds me back?*

Questions are important and being still, patient, and receptive to receiving the answers is even more important. When it comes to our self-love journey, it's important to consistently ask the questions that allow us to assess how we live out the Five Commandments of Self Love. Examples of questions that allow us to check in with our alignment of the commandments are as follows. *Am I honoring myself? Am I accepting my light and my darkness? Am I connected to my light in my darkness? Am I honoring my mind? Am I honoring my body? Am I honoring my spirit? Am I practicing forgiveness? Is there anything that I'm holding against myself? Is there anything that I am holding on against someone else? Are there any residual feelings of shame, guilt, bitterness, doubt, anger, or distressed for myself or others?* Life will always answer you, but you have to pose the questions. We can get so caught up in living that we don't even think about asking ourselves questions.

Consider the ways of a child. A child stays curious, consistently asking questions until about the age of nine or ten. They ask about the weather, love, why things are the way that they are. They ask questions about their family. They ask questions about why they look the way they look or why someone else looks different. They ask why the world works the way it does. The point is, they are persistently raising questions because they know they don't have the answer to everything. They know that they have a limited understanding. They know that if they have a question, they have access to some bank of information to provide them with the answer that satisfies their curiosity.

Something happens once we reach adolescence, where we either feel ashamed or too prideful to ask questions. We are discouraged from asking too many questions. We are told not to ask "dumb questions." We are encouraged just to think and not ask a question all the time. Every experience of discomfort that we are exposed to often dismantles our power to learn, be open and receive new information. It also disengages us from the process of transparency and vulnerability. When you ask a question, it is a sign of vulnerability because you are admitting that you don't know something. As adults, we live life not knowing the answers to life, but for some reason, we feel like we have to conduct ourselves in a way that makes it seem otherwise. We parade around as if we have all the answers and that we know what we're doing, when in reality, we don't; we're really just trying our best. If people felt more comfortable being open and asking questions to others around them, they would also be more comfortable in admitting that they don't completely understand themselves. They would ask the necessary questions to God or the universe that help them receive insight into how they show up in the world and how to maneuver this earthly experience.

When one gets to a stage of cognitive development and begins to assess who they are as an individual, this is the first major step to awakening. This is an awakening to navigating one's own truth. To be awakened is the ability to think critically and rationally about the implications of our decisions, and assess how much they are influenced by external circumstances or choices within the realm of our free will. It is very common to believe that we are acting freely and independent of influence when we are doing the very opposite. Everything we do or choose not to do is influenced by external circumstances. We are influenced by our primary caregivers, our families, friends, close relationships, places of work, communities, schools, faith or spiritual institutions, media, and our governments/political systems. Everything we see, hear, smell or touch impacts our perceptions of the world and ourselves.

At what point do you believe you started using the phrase self-love? Were you exposed to the concept of love or self-love first? Did you come to understand self-love because of how you functioned when you were in love?

It is proof of a higher level of consciousness when we understand that in order to have successful and healthy relationships with others and the world, we must be able to navigate our own internal dispositions. It is tough to genuinely appreciate and find the greatness or beauty in others if we don't see it in ourselves. Equally, it's' important to not idolize someone else's' talents or life's dispositions without being able to acknowledge our own strengths and talents. This is why connecting to the five commandments of self-love is helpful. As we become engulfed in and focused on each commandment, we become intentional about exploring the layering aspects of our beings. In being able to focus on our mind, bodies, and spirits as separate yet intertwining entities, along with the act of forgiveness, we grow in self-awareness and mindfulness.

In honoring our spirit and our mind, injecting the use of mindfulness or mentally expanding exercises do not only helps us regulate stress, but can also help us develop socio-cognitive skills as well as improve our emotional intelligence. In being able to honor and accept ourselves, we can then learn to do the same for others. Expressing empathy, compassion, and understanding for others allows us or leads us down a path of being able to do the same for ourselves. It has been founded that as adults, we can improve on what researchers call "socio-cognitive" and "socio-affective competencies" by learning to practice meditation, self-awareness, and mentally imagining ourselves in other's lives[iii].

Understanding ourselves helps us to understand people, and understanding people gives us the insight we need to understand ourselves. Everything and everyone is connected in some way, shape or form. Therefore, taking the time to really get to know, understand, and be gentle with ourselves is imperative. In knowing and understanding ourselves, we can then develop or hone in the internal resources that we need to thrive and continue to grow. In our self-awareness and self-knowledge, we can make more informed and intentional decisions in our lives. Knowing that we are honoring all parts of our being and living from a place of wholeness contributes to the notion of us doing our best. As we maneuver life doing our best, it gives us less opportunity to judge and hold a grudge against ourselves. Something that is important, so that we are not harboring unforgiveness.

I've learned that self-love ends up playing into the politics and dynamics of all relationships. When I reference relationship politics, I am referencing the spoken and unspoken rules that shape our relationships. Dynamics take into consideration balance of power, influence, leadership, playfulness, intimacy, boundaries, openness, communication, and expressiveness. I didn't even really know there was such thing as relationship politics until I began forging into my self-love journey. I became expressive about the journey and began sharing the tools that I found necessary to help me consistently operate in a place of self-love when in relationships with my loved ones. When I speak of relationships, I am speaking of family, friends, work, associates, and lovers. I learned that in my practicing self-love, it kind of goes against the grain. We are taught to compose ourselves and prioritize "respect." If in the practice of respect, I feel that my being is being diminished, that I'm being oppressed or subverted in any kind away, I'm supposed to just let it happen. I'm supposed to let it go because "you shouldn't hurt other people's feelings," that's rude. But what if these people are projecting hurtful ideals onto you? What if they're disrespecting you? What if they're crossing boundaries? What if they're making you feel uncomfortable? It's typically expected that you look past that and then continue to do so because it's the relationship politically correct thing to do.

According to these politics, it's not okay to shake things up; it's only okay to challenge people to a certain extent. In self-love, when you impose your own limits of comfort, aka boundaries, display how you honor and are accepting of yourself, others often feel uncomfortable, and as a result of their misguided discomfort, they want to shun you. They want to make you feel bad or guilty. They want to make you feel like you're overly selfish or overly self-indulged as if you don't care about them, as if you don't care about people. What I came to learn was that the real issue had little to actually do with my ability to practice self-love. That would be taking others' reactions way too personally. The truth is that most people don't have clear boundaries, so when they come in contact with someone who does and assertively imposes them, it's a foreign experience. The negative reactions that you may experience on your self-love journey are more about what your boundary practice represents for others.

In the beginning, it was a hard balance to practice. Being able to make sure someone else was just as comfortable as I am was difficult. In so many ways, I was used to compromising for the sake of the other person. The truth is that boundaries are not to create comfort for another. Boundaries are set to make sure you feel safe, comfortable, and healthy. When we lack healthy boundaries, we become over compromising and self-sacrificial. In practicing what I felt like was honoring myself, if in turn, someone else took offense, I realized that was not my problem. I had to learn how to own my own journey and leave issues that someone else has, to themselves because it has nothing to do with me. I could consider the possibility of my boundary triggering them; maybe my disallowance of their impeding on my space or my comfort, made them feel uncomfortable. Maybe me practicing self-love was a catalyst for how they feel, but how they feel has nothing to do with me. I became ok with discomfort as I remembered all the reasons why choosing me needed to be more of a priority.

First Comes Heartbreak

The average person is looking for love. Not from a place of desperation but a place of basic human need. Let's refer back to Maslow's hierarchy of needs. When we were younger, we are fascinated by this thing called love. Some of us step into it easier than others. Whereas some of us just really want it and don't even know where to begin.

When you're younger, and you're coming into yourself, you think about all the things that would make you into the ideal person, all the things that would make you into the ideal adult. A child or teenager doesn't know what it's like to be an adult; all they know is what they see. To them, being an adult means being in a relationship that seems cool, having a good job, making a good amount of money, and living in a nice place with a nice car. Those are experiences that they aspire to walk in. As we gain life experience, we realize all the things that we romanticized and put on a pedestal as a child are far from simple. One of the most complicated concepts that we learn about as we go thru life is romantic love. Love is easy when it's easy, and when it's hard it seems like it's the enemy.

If you've never had your heartbroken, I feel for you, I honor you, and I acknowledge the beauty and wholeness of your heart. Most of us have had our heartbroken. When you step into the experience that romantic love brings, you may enter with ideas of what you want to experience, how you want to feel, the outcomes of the relationship; you think about your future. You think about the hypothetical possibilities, and you focus on the positive, up until the point where you get to know the person on a deeper level and experience conflict with them. When conflict arises, or unfavorable habits and patterns emerge, you begin to consider the very opposite.

You may question your relationship and the compatibility with the person. You begin to consider how your relationship may end; you may even consider how that other person can hurt you. Thru all the millions of thoughts that one can consider about their relationship, you never can truly contemplate and comprehend how you would feel should and if your heart would ever be broken.

When the completion of a relationship occurs, depending on the attachment and depth of the relationship, we experience heartbreak. It feels like the ground has been taken out from under you. When you experience heartbreak, you may question who you are. You question your decisions. You question the relationship that you had. When you experience heartbreak, some of the basic things that used to bring you joy seem like things you want to stay away from because now, the very things that you did with your lover become reminders of that time.

Emotionally, the experience of heartache is equivalent to what's experienced during major loss and grief. In heartbreak or heartache, we are grieving the loss of a connection. We are losing a part of our identity. We are losing routine. We are experiencing the transition into a new version of our future, the future that no longer involves our partner.

Loss tends to bring about reflection. We replay our life choices. When we take a step back from any experience, we're able to gain insight in a way that is difficult to do while in the circumstance. This is why the say hindsight is 20/20. It is often going thru the darkness and walking into light when we consider that we were ever in the dark to begin with. In the existence of opposition, it is common to experience awareness after something ends, or is removed from our lives. When breathing without obstruction is normal, you don't realize how valuable and comfortable it is until you're sick, and your sinuses are flared up. You don't realize how comfortable it is to walk freely until you injure a part of your leg/foot or become sore from a workout.

We don't realize our excess or deficiency in self-love until we assess any destructive patterns, behaviors, relationships, and self-dialogue. We don't realize that we lacked self-love until we experience an interaction that depletes us from an inner strength, which we intuitively know exists. It's about having an experience that highlights our lack of alignment with our values or our perception of ourselves. It is often after a series of negative experiences within a relationship in which we experienced manipulation, control, or being taken advantage of; then, we see that we gave up our power or devalued ourselves, which allows us to honestly say, I need to love myself more.

People we choose to surround ourselves with, and the relationships we have, are the mirrors to who we really are. The people we attract and are attracted to provide us with a reflection of different parts of us. They show us our potential, our strengths, our gifts, our blind spots, our areas of opportunity, our downfalls, our limits in thinking, our success, our insensitivities, our gaps in understanding, and most importantly, our insecurities. When someone we are in relationship with does or says anything, it either resonates with us or makes us uncomfortable. The words and behaviors that resonate with us are a reflection of alignment or conflict with our values, principles, and beliefs. The things that make us uncomfortable does not only provide a mirror of our values, principles, and beliefs but also reveal our ability to be discerning, selective and intentional of the way we live our lives.

It seems that romantic relationships are the biggest mirrors of all because not only do they show us what we like within ourselves; they show us what we feel our worth is. They reveal to us the perception of our value. They show us how secure or insecure we are. They show us how dependent or independent we are. They show us our fears. They show us our insecurities. They show us our strengths. They show us our ability to establish, manage and honor boundaries. They show how selfless or selfish we can be. We get to see who we are when challenged and uncomfortable. We see the culmination of our greatest intrapersonal assets and our deepest wounds. We see the dealt with issues that are remnant of our relationships with our parents, or key figures in our lives. Whatever comes to surface while in a relationship often leaves marks on us. Most importantly, they show us our ability to express how we feel about ourselves and how we hold others accountable for treating us in a way that affirms such acknowledgment.

Heartbreak and heartache can change us. It is something about the disappointment or the completion of romantic relationships that seemed to set off a mental and emotional chain reaction within us. Because being in love and staying in love become so intertwined into our identities, as well as the social norms that come to define our value, we attach so much of who we are to the depths and length of our romantic relationships. Our relationships are really a mirror of who we are at a particular stage in life. We don't often perceive relationships as being tools of insight into who we are and where we are in a specific stage of life; we entrust that the success of a relationship actually adds or diminishes our self-worth. Many individuals actually embark on a dangerous and self-deprecating cycle in which they decide to withhold love from themselves because of what has occurred in their relationship.

Let's explore the complexity of romantic relationships. The most complex dynamic that can be present is those that exist in relationships marked by unhealthy or abusive behaviors. If I let you hurt me repeatedly, my allowance of your behavior is not reflective of my ability to stay committed no matter the "mistakes" or "growing pains" that you go thru; it is a reflection of how comfortable and deserving of pain I feel I am. My tolerance of your behavior, which in the right state of awareness I could deem as disrespectful or dishonorable, is reflective of the pain tolerance that I choose to endure. I personally choose pain to look like XYZ; therefore, I will teach you and affirm your learning of my pain tolerance. Essentially, if I can disrespect or dishonor myself up till a level 8, you too have permission to reflect such behavior up until it reaches a level where I am too uncomfortable and is forced to walk away. This is the narrative that is often followed when anyone stays in an unhealthy or abusive relationship.

In supporting domestic violence survivors in the past, I learned that everyone has a breaking point. For some survivors, it was broken bones, and for others, it was one blow to their face or a verbal threat of harming a family member or child. Relationships that are marked with any type of abuse (physical, psychological, verbal, or financial), neglect, or manipulation, are really about power and control. These are the relationships that are mentally difficult to walk away from because one is literally stuck in a vortex. If the control dynamics are really subtle, it makes it even more difficult to step out of. It's difficult to really see the totality of the danger being caused or experienced. It's often not until one can remove themselves from an abusive, toxic, or generally unhealthy conversation that they really gain the insight to assess, not only how unhealthy the relationship was, but also, all the ways they did not honor themselves. We begin to consider and realize how we can move forward in life to do so.

What I've learned about heartbreak is that you cannot get so blinded by what you perceive to be a failure of a relationship, which gives away your power to choose what you deserve. Often after "failures," people lose trust in themselves. I say "failure" because this word is really a matter of perception. When something ends, especially not in a way you hoped, you look at it as a failing circumstance as opposed to a lesson, blessing, or experience providing you with clarity on your life path.

In light of this failure, we also get slightly disconnected from our strengths because we may get in a place of deprecation. When we're disconnected from who we are, what matters, what we need, and especially what we want, we settle. Not only do we settle, but we convince ourselves that we are deserving of circumstances that don't honor us. That's why after some heartbreaks, we can travel down a road of empty relationships.

After what I perceived to be a series of unhealthy relationships, I decided to embark on my self-love journey to unlock what existed within me, which seemed to attract these circumstances constantly. Frankly, I wanted to make sure that I would never attract the type of relationship that I previously experienced. But what I realized is that while embarking on my journey, I unconsciously developed a victim and helplessness mentality. I began to analyze and consider my experiences thru a lens of being constantly misused or wronged. Due to my experiences from my romantic relationships, I developed a sense of fear in having a relationship, along with distrust in myself, in my ability to accurately choose a partner to experience a healthy and whole relationship. In reality, what was revealed taught me that I wasn't solely a victim. Yes I was wronged, but I also had a hand in harming others.

As an analytical and self-aware person, I said ok, Tiffany, you didn't ask for what has happened, but how did this happen again? Fool me one, shame on you. Fool me twice, shame on me. Fool me three times, girl, you better go to therapy, do some journaling and get to the root of the issue. I explored dimensions of myself that had laid hidden in repression or in pure unawareness. The challenge in this work was me believing that if I just "fixed" what was in me that was "broken" and attracting these healthy dynamics, I could prevent history from repeating itself. I believed that I could ensure my protection, as well as the occurrence of any unnecessary ills that come with troubled relationships. However, as I progressively worked on healing the wounds created from my past relationships, I learned some very valuable truths. Not only did I have major control issues, but I realized that my control issues were giving me a false idea around what I could control in reference to my relationships. No matter how whole, repaired or empowered I became, I realized that I could not ultimately control other people's actions; I could never totally avoid heartbreak because at the end of the day, someone choosing to do something without regards to how it would impact me, has nothing to do with me.

That's what heartbreak taught me on my self- love journey. That despite being in a relationship with

45

another, my relationship with myself will always matter most. If I stay focused on honoring myself, staying aligned with my values, and what matters to me, everything will fall into place. How someone chooses to show up in a relationship has less to do with me and more to do with them. I can only control myself and how I choose to show up. I often attribute my evolved acceptance to my own work, but the work I've done with my life coach. She has supported me in remembering that I can operate in grace, compassion, and acceptance, for others and as well as for myself.

Being with a partner that decides to put themselves before you has nothing to do with you; that is the agency that they are permitted to have. Sometimes, them putting themselves first is practicing healthy boundaries and self-care, and other times, it looks like engaging in behaviors they know would feel dishonoring or disrespectful to the relationship. Once I accepted that others have the freedom to choose themselves, I focused less on the actions of my partners that I once deemed selfish, accepted their humanness, and was able to reflect on the beauty, gifts, and growth that came from my relationship. Every circumstance has the potential to be a gift and offer something for you to take away; you can take away something about yourself or about the world.

Thru healing and re-connecting to the fact that aside from behaviors or decisions, which hurt or dishonored me, I recounted why I chose those men. For who I was, I chose what I felt like was good or good enough at that time. My present self shifted from feeling hurt and perceiving myself as a victim, to being empowered, and operating from a place of grace and forgiveness towards my younger self for the decisions she made. Evidently, no matter how ill-informed or distorted my understanding of healthy dynamics, at the time, I did my best. At the time, there was a beauty, strength, curiosity, and attraction that drew me to these men, and motivated me to choose them. Connecting to the power of my choice and the gift of the relationships reignited my confidence in myself and my ability to choose a partner that serves me.

This is why the self-love journey isn't black and white. It isn't just a matter of learning to accept yourself. As mentioned, the work you do on yourself is very much reflected in your ability to interact with others. Just as I learned to accept the duality and multidimensionality of my being, I learned to grant the same grace to someone else. If I know that I can walk in confliction, ambiguity, or hypocrisy, so can someone else. I've learned to accept that in my duality, I never have the intention of harming someone; however, I do tend to hurt or negatively impact others. What feels authentic and honest to me can be harsh, inappropriate or hurtful to others. Sometimes, people don't want honesty the way you want to serve it. Sometimes people want to hear what makes them feel better, even if that is a half-truth, or not speaking the truth at all.

It was in this epiphany that I realize despite how great, wonderful, aligned, powerful, or whatever attributes I believed my previous partners had at the time, the reality was; there existed various other attributes in there dualism. There existed insecurity, selfishness, irresponsibility, dishonesty, fear, hurt, and that was just their truth. Being able to not define experiences or people by a specific set of actions is something that's really hard for us to do with humans, but if we're talking about acceptance, we must learn to accept the reality of the spectrum human experience.

We must learn to accept the reality of how other people choose to live their life and not ascribe our worthiness based on how someone else treats us. Since we know that heartbreak has the power to affect our self-love journey, let's consider how the complete experience is processed. As life is 10% what happens to us and 90% how we respond, most of our response is based on our perception and believed locust of control. One's ability to activate or connect to resilience and come back from an emotionally or mentally challenging event is often connected to their internal resources, optimism, acceptance and support systems.

In efforts to focus on our growth, it's impactful to acknowledge, accept, and honor our emotions, but also take a step back and zero in on the lessons learned. Because separation from another can affect the lens of how we look at ourselves, it would be best if we objectively identified lessons, took the joy or pleasantness of the relationship for what it was, and literally leave the relationship in the past. Someone's inability to love you the way you want or need to be loved is not an indicator of your ability to be loved. Someone's lack of honesty in a relationship because of time, distance, communication or intimacy, is not an indicator of your ability to be loved. Someone's lack of love, divisiveness of love, or decision to end your relationship, is not indicative of your worth or value. We allow these experiences to shake up our world so much and to shake up how we perceive ourselves. In self-love, we must accept not only ourselves, but the circumstances that we're dealt with in life, and do our best. We must do our best to walk thru them, walk over them, overcome them, and continue living, thriving, and being the best version of ourselves.

Realizing You Feel Incomplete

People unintentionally spend their lives in search of people, places, and things to fill up the voids that exist within them. They wonder why they are never satisfied. They pursue relationships that help them feel better about themselves. They purchase items and pursue a lifestyle that makes them feel as if they have high value because of their mere affiliation. People set goals and go after accolades, only to be met with an underwhelming lack of gratification when it comes to their life. The undiscovered, unrealized and unconscious reality is that they actually feel incomplete.

I sincerely believe that the catalyst for intentionally embarking on a journey of self-love comes from a realization, acknowledgment and admission that you do not fully love yourself. Let's sit with that for a moment because to admit something like this takes a lot of courage, and most importantly, vulnerability. Vulnerability is extremely difficult when we are used to others' judging and criticizing us, or if we are the harsh judges and criticizers. *What would it mean if we were to be honest, and open ourselves up to admit such a thing?*

For some people, they believe they either love themselves, or they don't, but the human experience is more complex than that; we must consider our spiritual and psychological experiences as well. There can be aspects of your being that you love and honor, and others that you feel repelled and repulsed by. What is important to note is; which side does the weight stand? *If we were to pull out a scale, would it fall in favor of love, or fall in favor of not loving yourself?* That is important.

Looking back on the source that leads us to feel incomplete, void, empty, or not enough can provide challenge. It can be rooted in your own sense of self or have been imposed by someone else, but it's important to ask the question, *when did I begin to feel incomplete?* At some moment, on the heels of the ending of a relationship, thru the eyes or story of someone else, while listening or watching a motivational person, you have a moment of realization. It's not always clear because being satisfied with, embracing, and accepting certain parts of your being can provide an illusion of you believing that you are "fine," but the revelation really comes in the spontaneous, quiet, and still moments are powerful. These are moments when you're alone or when you are challenged by the universe to interact with someone who is a mirror to and for you. It will be a moment in which something or someone will allow you to explore much deeper and realize that there has been a sense of incompleteness within you because you see it in them, or something they say resonates with you in a way that brings these insecurities to awareness.

It is an essential cognitive function for our brain to create narratives and fabricated details of truths that do not exist. Our brains need the whole story, so when there is a portion of the story missing, our brain devises something that would make sense. When we do not feel whole, or when we do not feel our best, we overcompensate by taking on identities, acquiring material possessions, and finding coping mechanisms to distract us from the truth. Our minds have received enough information to categorize what stimuli or associations create a sense of value. Based on what you were socialized to believe, there are certain associations that you would have with power, value, worthiness, respect, etc. The established cognitive associations drive us to reach for and be close to these people, places, and things that temporarily boost our esteem, or grant us access to relationships that allows us to feel complete.

The challenge comes when we decide to actually look within and examine the truth. *What is the motivation behind the drive of attaining or being associated with a particular person, place or item?* Being able to connect the motivation to an actual emotion will give you the insight and power to introspectively reflect as to where you are and what you really need. The key to understanding what is driving your behavior lies in understanding your thoughts and your emotions. This is why acknowledging your emotion is so fundamental to building a relationship with yourself, and understanding 'who you are.' Emotions provide information. When you feel any sense of emptiness, lack, deficiency, deficit, shame, or guilt about your truth, don't only look at the cause but also why you've been living in resistance from owning, facing and walking in your truth. *Why are you feeling the way you're feeling? What are you hiding from?*

The truth can always be difficult to explore and interact with. Of course, it can be difficult digging up and bringing to light information that felt or feels easier to suppress. It will pose a challenge, but more than anything, it will give you freedom and power of choice. Instead of letting your emotions, insecurities, or negative core beliefs run you and guide your life, you get to choose intentionality, self-awareness, and self-love to choose how you want to live your life powerfully. As you bring more to surface, you will uncover and explore aspects of your identity that you possibly did not know existed.

Because many people spend their lives living for others, fitting in social norms, and essentially hiding from themselves, many lack insight into the multitude of layers that comprises their identity. Self-love is about accepting and honoring who you are, so with that, having insight into how you became to be who you are, and how you develop into who you want to be is of extreme value. Identity development can be a complex concept because there are so many variables that shape who we are. At the root of identity, psychologists have theorized that we are partly influenced by nature, which is our genetic disposition, and partly influenced by nurture, the environment in which we are socialized. There are a fraction of our traits that are passed down genetically from our parents that make up our general temperament. In Psychology, these basic personality profiles are defined as the "Big 5" [iv]and they are neuroticism, extraversion, openness, agreeableness, and conscientiousness.

The other aspects of our identity are largely shaped by our environment and lived experiences. Our self-developed identities, as well as our identity in relationship to groups like our family, geographic communities, ethnic or cultural identities, and so much more. Think about groups and subcultures that shape us like musical genres, sports teams, college/universities, hobby groups, social clubs/organizations, political affiliations, professional associations, languages, astrology, gender, and affiliations of our personal values, beliefs, worldly perspectives and so many other influences. So we have genetics, family, belief systems, external groups, but we must not forget one of the biggest culprits – media. In recent years, media has come to impact identity reportedly more intensely than ever before.

With all these factors constantly at work, gaining a sense of who you are can really be about unlearning what you've been taught. It could be stepping away from the heaviest influences, to check in with yourself about true alignment. We can ask the question; *do any of the factors that have shaped my identity add to or create the experience of me feeling deficient or void?*

Taking on Identities That Distract Us From the Truth

There are very few absolutes in life; therefore, what one knows to be "the truth" is a very relative concept. Truth, in many ways, is relative because it can be subjective. For Instant, two people from different countries and cultures can look at the same painting and interpret it differently, can have the same "ethnic" cuisine and have different experiences with it, or be told the same words and interpret it differently. Both individuals have different truths, so it is problematic to believe that both individuals will operate the same.

A belief in any truth can lead one person, group, community, or nation to live a particular lifestyle according to a specific set of values and beliefs. What you have to understand is that your perception of the world is not the only perception. There is no one way to live life. We grow up in silos, and as much as we believe that people around us think, act, walk and talk similarly, we often learn that once we step outside of those silos, we find that there are people that walk, talk, think, and speak differently. It seems like such is a concept of common sense, but the sense you believe is common, can be non-existent to another.

When it comes to our own identity, consider how strong of an influence other people's perceptions and other people's truths have on us. From the time that we are born, we are bombarded with ideas of what it takes to be a man or woman, but we don't learn that gender identity is a spectrum, and that there are no absolute clear ways how one "should" act. Beyond being socialized into gender norms, we learn about socially acceptable behaviors, lifestyles, and life pathways. What we are most exposed to becomes our understanding of the world. What we are exposed to creates the labels.

Generally, our understanding of the world remains limited until we start asking questions, and we realize there is actually more that we don't know than that in which we do. Not only do we have a limited understanding of the world, but we may, unfortunately, know little when it comes to our identity. We often do not know how to separate what is authentically us and what has been heavily influenced by our environment. The result is that we unknowingly take on an identity that does not come from within; it does not reflect who we really are. These pseudo identities disconnect and distract us from our true selves because we put ourselves in the boxes, in the holes, and in the confinement of the constructions that have been forced on us, and they take away from authentic living experience.

Social constructions can lead you to suppress and doubt your emotions and thoughts. Affiliations with groups that stand upon certain values may cause you to experience dissonance when a value that you personally identify with, which may differ from a said group is challenged, but you don't have a solidified enough connection with yourself to honor that discomfort, and step out on your own. We minimize our emotions, instead of letting them reveal what is going on with our inner being because of the identities we're hiding behind.

When one spends their life growing into what and who they believe they should be, it is difficult to step away from that life to explore who they really are; shed that previous identity, and embrace the new one. Consider the previous section that explored the notion of wearing masks. Masks or false identities, keep us separated from ourselves. It is almost easier to live life in a false identity, rather than to stand in our truth. Standing in who we really are, takes a lot of courage, constant acknowledgment, acceptance, and accountability.

Acquiring Material Possessions

The western world often believes that one is defined by their material possessions and assets. There is so much emphasis on acquiring "more." We are bombarded with advertisements that constantly stimulate a desire to obtain more of anything and upgrade to the newer or bigger version of what already exists. Everything is about excess. If you are not on-trend, then you are out of touch. You may rarely get anyone to speak those specific words; however, it's implied by the consumption trends, revolving debt, and popularity of people, words, images, and content that promote the lifestyle of consumption. The love of lavishness is absolutely not a new concept; however, the pressure and resulted shame that one experiences if they are without it are more prevalent than ever.

When you don't know how to define yourself or when you don't know what makes you unique, you will look for outside validation and circumstances to project to the world 'who you are.' When you are disconnected from yourself, you will seek people, experiences, and objects to fill the space that exists in you. It is easy to lean on things to cover up who you are or the insecurities that you have about yourself. By emphasizing what one has, they get to lean on symbols of success, value, or importance. This mindset that sets value on possessions often begins in childhood.

When you grow up without something, or you're made fun of because you don't have something, and if you have an idea that you are not enough without things, the romanticization of having more begins. Often times, young people become adults who set goals for the type of possessions that they want. They believe that those possessions are not only going to make them happy, but those possessions will make them appear a certain way to others. The belief is that what they will grant them access to certain resources and networks. It will grant them access to their happiness. Anyone that has amassed a large amount of wealth and possessions can tell you that acquiring "things" does not make one happy and actually does not define a person. We do not understand, or we tend to forget that who we are and who we want to be is an internal process of development. We are too willing to disassociate ourselves from such a deep and intimate understanding of self and rely too much on the superficial.

There's a perception that those who live a life with an overflow of material possessions and endless privileges are "living the life" because it seems like they have everything. However, it's not what someone has that draws you to them. It's not people's possessions that make them seem noteworthy people. It's really about the charisma that some of these people have, even if it is engineered. They have something special about them. They might be givers. They might be people who intentional focus on how they impact the world. An observer might be inspired by the words of an influencer. All in all, because there's a misunderstanding or misinterpretation of the kind of light that shines from within them, it's easy to overestimate the importance of the things they have and assume how much those possessions matter.

What you have does not define you. What you have is not who you are. What you have is just a token and a remnant of your life, but at your depth at your core, what lies in your soul – that is who you are. The credentials and the accolades that you collect thru your life are a part of you; they are part of your story; they are not your story. Your accolades and credentials are minute reflections of who you are because they share a story about your goals, passions, talents, and skills. They may tell a story about influences that have shaped your pathway. No one can ever take away your accolades or your accomplishments; however, they do not define you. You are more than what you do. The essence of you cannot be limited to the possessions that you obtain on your life's journey.

Finding Coping Mechanisms

What you do when you feel stressed, depressed, angry, irritated, sad anxious, envious, jealous, or merely out of control? What activities do you find yourself engaging in? Do you seek to "numb" yourself? Do you try to detach and distance yourself from your emotional experience? How do you deal with life?

The answer to these questions can provide insight into your relationship with yourself. Whatever you do in response to stress or events that challenge imbalance, we call it a coping mechanism. Your ability to use the healthy and safe mechanism as opposed to maladaptive and unsafe mechanisms is what's referred to as coping skills.

In this section, I will explore coping mechanisms in response to any type of stressor but will focus on those that are used in trauma responses.

Stressors are stimuli that technically cause your cortisol levels to rise. Cortisol is one of the many hormones that our body produces, and its production typically occurs when out, senses connect to some sense of danger, threat, or discomfort. Biologically, we are built to manage and respond to major stressors such as childbirth, violence, overt anger, and predators. As the human experience has evolved, so has the type of stressors that exist. Most of us no longer live in nomadic, hunter-gatherer societies, so we're not looking out for external threats like animals or having to challenge other humans for survival physically, at least not like our ancient ancestors. Unfortunately, there are many threats that people face every day. There are people living in circumstances where they are challenging other humans for their livelihood. We have stressors due to technology, transportation, political systems, finances, social injustices, interpersonal dynamics, and so much more.

The reality is that stressors happen. We experience stress even when we don't feel stressed. How we interact with the stressors is important when it comes to our overall wellness, but also our relationship to ourselves. When it comes to our relationship to ourselves, self-love, and coping mechanisms, it's important to be mindful of any activities that allow you to honor yourself and where you at while being mindful of staying distant from anything that would compromise your ability to honor yourself.

There are coping mechanisms that can be considered healthy and self-honoring, and others that can be unhealthy and maladaptive. There are types of coping mechanisms that are overt and others that are subtle. There are mechanisms that behaviors are based on activity and others based in response. At the heart of the matter, coping is about regulating the emotional experience. When we experience a stressor, it elicits an emotional response, which we naturally seek to "manage," "deals with," or "repress."

Emotions like shame, guilt, anger, sadness, and loneliness can often lead us to numbing behaviors. People seek comfort, validation, or release in something that minimizes their true emotional experience. The most popular mechanisms are food (whether restricting, binging or overeating), chemical substances like drugs or alcohol, sex or meaningless romantic relationships, and impulsive spending. These activities are not unhealthy in and of themselves; what makes them unhealthy is the intention that the user has in using them. If they are intended to help you disconnect with yourself or reality, they may be a problem. There is no true freedom in running away or hiding from the truth. The more you hide, the more you get comfortable with disconnection from self, which in turn leads to these behaviors having control over you to the point of developing an addiction and other mental illness; your ability to live without these activities become impaired.

More subtle mechanisms include behaviors like self-sabotage, silencing self, pushing away others emotionally, withdrawing from others, isolation, passive-aggressive communication, or criticizing/demeaning/belittling others. It is common that when we become dysregulated emotionally, it impacts how we communicate and interact with others. These behaviors erode, poison, and strain our relationships.

Whether you are someone who leans on overt behaviors, or more subtle, it's always important to explore the psychological benefit you're getting. Consider if you engage in behaviors that put you in harm's way, separate you from your support system, or even cause you to lose contact from who you are. *How can you honor yourself when there are distractions keeping you from being in alignment with who you really are?*

Getting a hold on coping mechanisms can get even more complicated for those who are trauma survivors. Beyond normal stressors, trauma survivors are constantly finding ways to ensure comfort, safety, and security. As much as the day to day stressors can be harmful to our well-being, the experience of trauma has an extra layer of complexity.

There are uncontrollable life experiences that compromise our sense of safety, wholeness, and ability to cope with our circumstances. Some events and periods in our lives can be so damaging, that they leave psychological footprints on our functioning. The more self-aware we become, we get to step into the awareness of our fears, limiting beliefs, unhealthy coping mechanisms, and feelings of void. When we experience what is known as trauma, the molecular functioning of our brains changes, in addition to the physiological responses we experience to stressors. Trauma can occur as a one-time event, a series of events, or over the course of time. When one experiences multiple traumas over a major period, this is known as complex trauma. The traumas can be related, such as someone who has experienced child abuse as well as abuse in subsequent romantic relationships, or the traumas can be unrelated. Those who experience what is known as complex trauma often suffer from psychological problems such as low esteem, self-hatred, substance abuse, depression, anxiety, self-destructive and risk-taking behaviors, revictimization, problems with interpersonal and intimate relationships, medical illnesses and despair[v].

In 1999, the Center for Disease and Control and Kaiser published results from a questionnaire-based study conducted randomly with Kaiser Patients. The study looked at the impact of Adverse Childhood Experiences, also known as ACES. The study posed yes or no questions to questionnaire takers, exploring the following experiences before the age of 18: physical neglect, emotional neglect, parental separation/divorce, incarceration of someone in the home, mental illness, substance abuse, mother treated violently, sexual abuse, physical abuse, and emotional abuse. Abuse could be witnessed or directly experienced. What they found was of the 17,000 participants; the more ACEs someone had, the higher their likelihood of risky behaviors, chronic illnesses, mental illness, unwanted pregnancies, infectious diseases, limited economic and vocational opportunities, and physical injury.

The experience of trauma leads us to experience intense levels of dysregulation, thus leading us to the environment, relationships, and circumstances that temporarily relieve the pain, but have long term impact. The experience of trauma causes our bodies to become imbalanced, and we engage in behaviors often times that may exacerbate the problems even more. Learning to honor where you are, learning to honor who you are, learning to essential what you need, is instrumental, but taking the necessary action actually honor yourself, your mind, your body, and your spirit leaves you empowered.

It is in our self-awareness that we hold power. Once we can recognize the need to change, the need to improve, or the need to elevate ourselves, it is only then can we assess where we are and begin to make plans to move forward. In self-love, it's easy to acknowledge what strengths we have, but it is not always easy to acknowledge our pain, our incompleteness, and where it comes from. If you are a survivor of any kind of trauma, but especially complex, you must understand that how you choose to cope with life or what patterns you've developed to cope with life is really important for you to pay attention to. *Do your coping mechanisms make you susceptible to more traumas? Do your coping mechanisms symbolize or draw parallel to trauma that you have previously experienced?*

Sometimes we respond to life in a very reactionary manner. We respond in a way that is not intentional and comes from a place of unconsciousness. We react from a survival instinct. We react from a place of fear. We react from a place of deficit. We react from a place of compromised safety and groundedness because of our experience with trauma. Often, when individuals lack the tenacity to embark on a self-love journey or to put forth the effort in self-care or self-acceptance, it's not because they are lazy or disinterested. It is often because their internal resources for resilience and self-nurturing have been compromised because of their life experiences, and they may not feel the emotional or mental capacity to shift their thoughts and behaviors.

When a compromised sense of safety is your normal, it's difficult to connect to an experience in which you're not required to be in control, or in a fight, flight or freeze mode. When your main narrative is "I am not safe," "everything is not ok," "I must stay aware" or even "Life is too intense, I can't stand this," the consideration of an opposite experience can be difficult to grasp. However, once you realize that your normalized experience of feeling unsafe, incomplete, detached, hopeless, depressed, is your constant state, then it is up to you to search for and gather the tools that you need to help you heal from your wounds. Gather what you need to help you release the negative thoughts and perspectives about yourself and/or to help you release the negative narratives that you had regarding your place, importance, and impact in this world. This process will take time. It takes time to realize that you do matter and that you do belong to something bigger than yourself. It takes time to realize that you can learn how to honor yourself even though people have been dishonoring you all your life. It takes time for you to realize that the thoughts and feelings that you have of you not being enough, has nothing to do with you, but has been shaped by the projection of other individuals who have low esteem, who do not honor themselves, who do not love themselves, and who have probably experienced trauma in their own life. Don't rely on unhealthy coping mechanisms to comfort you. Learn to accept your truths, and develop positive coping skills to help you nurture, love, and empower yourself.

Desire for Change

Change is difficult. Thus, for one to take a step onto a different path, the pain of staying the same must outweigh the pain of change.

In addiction therapy, there is a concept called the stages of change. In this model of change, we see six stages that one would typically go thru to stay committed to breaking an addiction. The first stage is pre-contemplation. The second stage is contemplation. The third stage is planning. The fourth stage is action. The fifth stage is maintenance. The sixth and somewhat temporary stage is one of relapse. This is defined by action or period when a recovering addict is engaging in their addictive behavior after they've received an intervention. Because of the likelihood of relapse occurring, many behavioral therapists prefer for an addict to use the phrase, recovering addict. It ascribes a more free-flowing and generous label to someone's illness.

In looking at this framework, one can surely see that it is applicable beyond extreme addictive behaviors. There are habits that we all have, which classically wouldn't be labeled as dangerous in their existence; however, we know how much of a negative impact they can have on us. For accuracy, let's interchange the word addicted to constantly drawn to or overpowered by. We can be constantly drawn to neglecting our health, blaming and guilting ourselves when such accountability is out of context, being in environments that are compromising, toxic relationships, victimizing ourselves, and so much more. These are habits and patterns that we may either engage in repetitively or long term, whether conscious or unconscious of the fact.

Going into the deepest part of your soul and being able to smile at what you see is the sign of a revolutionary love affair. It's a love affair with yourself. It is proof that you can truly learn to come to terms with your truth and accept it. To face what once seemed dark and see its revelation as a lesson of opportunity and growth is a path only for the bravest of spirits. It takes sheer boldness and audaciousness to live a life of authenticity, transparency, and acceptance. It takes courage because it's gravely uncomfortable and difficult. To one day turn your head or your heart inside out with despair because of what you know to be true and then later embrace it all is freedom at its best. You have the freedom to take life by whatever arms you choose to. This acceptance is the path of self-love.

When you go thru a spiritual transformation that opens your mind and spirit, it can seem that the part of consciousness has a tough time comprehending the power that resides in you. It is the power to connect with God or power source and call things to pass with the

71

clear intention of their manifestation. The spiritual game is one of transparency, authenticity, acceptance, learning, and growing. The more you play the game, the higher you seem to rise, and the more effortlessly life seems to be. Your relationships, your conquests, your opportunities truly flow from a higher place. The higher the level of your frequency, the more connected to God you are, the more connected to yourself you are.

Commandment 1: Honor Thy Self

It All Begins With This

Every journey begins with a question. Typically asking one question leads to other questions. Our journey then becomes focused on asking and answering questions. Our journeys are tunnels of discovery. The more that we ask, the more we learn. Questions allow us to ponder and stay in curiosity about the answers that life can provide. When you ask a question and ponder anything, the Universe will always bring forth answers to you. The most impactful questions begin with why? I often find "why" as a prompting beginning to exploring how truth that is impacted by self brings one to their current state. When experiencing hurt or disappointment, especially repeatedly, one might ask: *Why does this keep happening to me? Why is this happening to me now? Why am I not where I thought I would be or want to be?* Do any of these questions sound familiar? Being impeccable with our words, and the way we ask questions is also important. Making sure questions are open-ended, subjective, and not filled with judgment is really important. The above questions could be asked in different ways. *Why does this cycle keep appearing in my life? Why is this current circumstance occurring? What are the healthy and unhealthy trends/patterns in my relationship?*

It is at the point that we stop looking for answers to questions like these that we stop learning.
Taking on the curiosity of a child and applying the wisdom of an adult can support our pursuits of growth, transformation, and self-love. In our pursuit of self-love, our proverbial question is; *what is love?* Secondly, we can ask *what is self-love?* We then may ask, *how can I learn to love myself?* Or *how can I love myself more?* The last two questions are those that would be posed to me very often. I would have women from time to time say to me, "Tiffany, I feel like I need help; I need to learn how to love myself. How do I learn how to practice self - love? The first two questions I would typically ask are, *what does self-love mean to you? What are the indications that you are not practicing self-love?* The definition that we will constantly be exploring is that of love itself. As a result, what will happen is that our relationship and understanding of love will constantly

shift, and we can constantly assess it in our shifting understanding of love if our understanding of self-love can shift. Love is the root of each of the five commandments. Each commandment is formed so that you may understand what it means to Love. Honor thy self is the first commandment and the foundation for them all.

Imagine a tree of the Oak species which has been planted and nourished in the woods of Humboldt, California, whose roots have run deep into the Earth for 35 years. One day, this beautiful creation of nature decides that it wants to survive, but wants to cut off its roots and become a Pine. What it does not realize is that it cannot survive without its roots. It could never become Pine because that is not its nature. The Oak can never be what it wants by rejecting all that has nurtured it. All of the animals that used it as shelter; all of the beautiful summers, springs in which its leaves blossomed; all of the harsh winters and the autumns which it has endured have all created it to stand tall for 30 years. The Oak was created for a purpose. It has become what it has become because of all that it weathered. Nothing matters more than the Oak being what its' meant to be, just for the purpose of Being.

In understanding how you can honor yourself, you must look inward, and ask the questions that shed light on your connection with yourself. *How have you processed hurt? How have you processed disappointment? How have you processed failure? How have you dealt with missed opportunities? How have you processed dismantled relationships? Are they just occurrences of the past? Or have you actually taken into consideration how they've affected you?*

Who you are isn't just defined by who you decide to be at this very moment. It is the collection of moments, interactions, experiences, ideas, environments, and people that have shaped you. Everything from your personal style to your sense of hygiene and your view of education, to your views of and relationship with politics, environmentalism, health, relationships, family, spirituality, and more. It can also be your definition of love, the patterns in which you choose to, and not to love.

All that you are, your likes, dislikes, fears, and enjoyment all have a root. For you to understand who you are and what you can do to be involved in your growth process, you must explore the roots. In exploring the roots, you will face some difficult truths. Truths that may shake you up; distract or disrupt your current state of being. Truths that expose the true nature of some of your major relationships and shine a light on what is considered menial or insignificant relationships in your life. Truths that will bring clarity to who you are. Truth that breeds accountability.

When you arrive at a point in which you actively search for the answers to questions about yourself and life, you will find the world to be a different place. It's almost like a re-wiring of your mind happens. Asking questions invigorates the critical thinking, analytical, and solutions-focused areas of your brain. You begin to operate in a world in which you now see that everything and everyone is connected, connected to the extent that everything affects one another. You may even become more open as to the sources from which the answers to your question come from. The truth is that there is infinite intelligence around us; there is an abundance of teachers to provide us with insight into ourselves and life if we are open to learning. We can learn from our own reflections, just as much as we can learn from teachers outside of us. Teachers are everywhere. Teachers are found in others, older, younger, and the same age. Teachers are historical events. Teachers are family, past, and present. Teachers are music, traditions, religious texts, and other markers of culture. Teachers are animals, plants, climates, seasons, and other occurrences in nature. The infinite intelligence that exists within and around is a form of energy. Energy is neither created nor destroyed; it is merely transferred.

This is why connecting to all that has impacted you is vital. When we train our minds and sense of consciousness to see everything as a lesson, piece of information, or extension of us, we develop more patience, tolerance, compassion, gentleness, insight, and understanding for ourselves and those around us. This is what it means to honor yourself, honoring all energies, experiences, and relationships. To honor is to recognize. As a transformational being, recognition is a simple force that continues to ignite the process. In honoring yourself, you take apart the many layers of your being while appreciating the wholeness of the masterpiece that is you. Often, when we get to a place of reflection, it tends to be due to an experience that has aroused judgment, intense emotion, or a sense of dissatisfaction. We ask ourselves questions stemming from all the whys that mark our past.

Choosing to walk boldly thru the world is a big deal. It's a monumental task that many are afraid to do. The fear to be one's true self is one of the greatest enemies that most of us choose not to face. Out of fear of judgment and exclusion, the desire to feel accepted by others, unfortunately, overshadows our contentment to accept ourselves. *What is it about vulnerability, transparency, and truth that keep so many beings from embracing who they are?*

As you ponder on how you can better honor yourself, take time to ponder, *in what ways do I neglect, reject, or belittle myself?* Literally ask, *in what ways do I not or am I not honoring myself?* Honoring yourself is a moment by moment and day by day process. It is not an act or way of living that comes easy. At times, you making decisions or operating from a place of honor, and acceptance may be easier than others. Honoring yourself comes up in internal dialogue and in day to day actions. Honoring yourself comes up when you are interacting with others. To honor yourself is to offer yourself unapologetic love, upliftment, and acceptance. To honor yourself is to walk thru the world, being mindful yet unapologetically you. To be unapologetic, you are to speak about and walk-in yourself without a persistent apology.

We apologize to appease others. In our apologies, we at times belittle ourselves. Some people constantly say, "I'm sorry," even if an apology is not warranted. This is often a reflection of a loud, critical voice that tells us, "You are wrong," "You are bad," "What's wrong with you?" "Now look at what you've done." People become over apologetic when they believe they don't deserve to take up space in this world, or they believe that their imperfections or mistakes are inexcusable. Something inside of you or someone outside of you has made you feel like you are "sorry" and constantly mistaken. As a response to critical inner narratives like this, set intentions that support you in learning how to honor yourself. The daily intention that would support you to learn to honor yourself: be gentle with yourself.

Lessons in Self Love : The 4 A's

Acknowledgment, acceptance, accountability, and authenticity are essential to the experience of self-love. **Acknowledgment** of who you are is the first step. Much of our life is unintentionally committed to doing what we feel we need to do for others to see us. We spend our lives trying to prove ourselves to others. We perform to get grades, win competitions, win hearts, and be acknowledged by others. Insecurities are birth out of the internal experience of not feeling like we're enough. When we don't feel enough, we are driven towards behaviors and lifestyles that warrant us to be validated by outside sources. It drives our career choices. It drives what we feel like we need to do to attract romance. It drives the social circles we join. It drives the decisions we make around family planning. The issue with this constant drive for motivation, is that we lose our true selves, creating a life that is essentially for others to approve of.

Within this complex journey, are the additional experiences people may have that shape these seeking approval behaviors; which is frequently, impacted by the words of others. When we experience the critiques of others, we are subscribing to a narrative that says we are not enough. So not only do we seek validation to make us feel worthy, but we secretly seek validation to prove to these people that we are good enough.

Take into consideration an unhealthy transformation process cloaked as empowerment, called "the revenge body." It's a popular idea that one will seek to attain a body type or physical appearance that would create envy of their ex-lover. In order to take back one's power, the sweetest revenge is looking better than one did when they were with their ex. The general concept could be powerful, but it lies flat because it continues to play into the idea that who we are needs to be impacted by or will impact others. For sure, we live in a visually stimulated society, influenced heavily by the fashion and beauty industry. That, coupled with a generation that has dramatically impacted major growth in the fitness and health/diet industry, is reason enough to understand how simple it pressures that looking appealing is central to so many people's identities.

However, the truth is that if you are not truly content with who you are and don't work out whatever issues you have around loving another, no matter of aesthetics will matter. Your body is just a shell, but who you are on in the inside, the quality of your thoughts, and how you feel about yourself is the primary aspect of your being in need of transformation. External transformations only have a limited impact on a person.

In my work doing therapy with individuals who have eating disorders, I often see emotional pain, at the core of many with illness; the pain that comes with helplessness or rejection. Clients trying hard to avoid the pain that would be experienced, from a body that is typically not accepted in society — the pain of not feeling enough. The pain of rejection and need to find a way to soothe themselves. I would state that many do not see themselves beyond their bodies, and it's very difficult to establish and maintain a relationship with themselves. In the midst of it all, food is just a tool. Whether body image is at the center or not of one's eating disorder, there is a sense hopeless, despair, and sheer disappointment in self. There is little acceptance, and there often tends to be much shame, anger, and emotional disconnection or apathy. Many can be on the verge of dying, reaching for the body type they believe would grant them a life of acceptance, love, and success. The irony is, people can attain the body they want, and still not believe it's not good enough or still not believe that they are good enough.

One must learn to **acknowledge** who they are. Exploration of self includes understanding one's values, core positive and maladaptive beliefs, key behavioral patterns, hobbies, interests, all the ways that you propel and prevent yourself from obtaining what you want, your communication style, emotional expression style, the roles you play, your perceived strengths and areas of opportunities, and literally how you see yourself. You have to SEE yourself. Seeing yourself is the path to acknowledgment.

Once you can acknowledge yourself, then you take steps to accept who you are. This is why the first commandment of self-love is Honor Thyself. A tenant of honoring one 'self is actually to accept everything about yourself. In the realm of therapy, there is a concept of Radical Acceptance. Radical **Acceptance** is based on the practice of being able to be content with who you are and what exists without judgment and critique. It could seem like the antithesis of improvement and growth, but it is not. In radical acceptance, one is connected to their present self and the way their life is. When we are intensely fixed on changing, we subconsciously tell ourselves that there is a deficit, incompletion, and lack. Who we are is not enough. Our life is not enough. It creates an experience of sadness. It fuels comparison. It incubates admiration of something different to the point that we are always chasing after something. Consider how some people are never satisfied with who they are or who lack appreciation for what they have, what they've done, and who they've become, and what exists. Radical acceptance is the prescription for persistent dissatisfaction.

If you are a whole being, made up of 100% of you, and you choose to share the most likable 25% part of you, it does not mean you are fake or inauthentic, it means you're scared, not comfortable and not completely accepting of yourself. As you begin to see your true self, not just the self you want to share selectively, but who you would be without the extra chatter from yourself or external pressures of the society; the more truth you will see. As you see the truth, continue to walk in it. As you walk in it, you can choose how you move forward on your journey of acceptance.

Do not lie to yourself.

One of the greatest impediments to our own growth is our lack of willingness to accept our shortcomings and toxic cycles. We reject the idea that we could be wrong or could even improve. Stubbornness and pride are toxic, and they are contributing factors as to why we can be so wrapped up in lies, and continue to perpetuate the lies. When we choose to lie to ourselves, we're not even completely aware that we're lying. Others look at it as denial, a complete disregard, or a distancing from the truth.

You cannot accept the truth that you do not face. If you are lying to yourself about what you want, who you are, how you act, what your strengths and areas of opportunities are, what is keeping you from getting to know your next level, and what your greatest fears are, you may never really know the truth. You may never really get to a place where self-love can reign supremely.

Following acceptance is an action that presents a challenge for most, accountability. **Accountability** is about stepping into the truth about your role in the unfolding of your life. Accountability is about owning the decisions that have impacted your life, as well as the decisions you've made that have impacted others' lives. Accountability feels difficult for many because we've learned that accountability is most connected to critique, judgment, and blame. But it's anything but that. Unless there is an actual critique, judgment, and blame, most of the time, the wounded, insecure, afraid, and belittled child in within ourselves do not know how to process or sit in the discomfort of accountability. Our wounded selves interpret accountability as "being bad" or "being wrong." For one to know self, one must learn to accept the type of decisions they make, as well as the patterns of behaviors and thoughts that they operate in. Some behaviors and thoughts serve you, and others don't. Some behaviors and thoughts are helpful for our relationships, and others may be harmful. This is why accountability is important: owning our behaviors without judgment. Taking ownership and being gentle with ourselves as we move forward in our life. To accept yourself, you must learn to accept all of yourself.

It is important to note that the critical voice is the most dangerous aspect of practicing acceptance. For people who have a loud, critical voice, they are more apt to be harder on themselves and dig into themselves when they unearth difficult truths about themselves. A critical person can become overly fixated on "removing" or "eliminating" what they can perceive as deficiencies. Acceptance is not critiquing. It's not about harshness. It's not fixing you. If that is where you are, let's practice Radical Acceptance, and move forward intending to be gentle with self.

Lastly, there is authenticity. Authenticity is one of the indicators that self-love has actualized. It can almost feel impossible for someone to truly be authentic because of the heavy impact of social norms. Authenticity is one's ability to genuinely and unapologetically express and be themselves. It can be nerving to be truthfully honest and reveal the parts of you that others may have a problem with, may challenge, or even disagree with. The intersectionality of our identities leads us to be a part of multiple subcultures ruled by various norms. Often times, if you are not following a norm, or even a social trend, it can feel like you're alone. It can feel like you're an outsider. To be an outsider at times can cause fear, especially if you have any issues with acceptance. Yet this is why the mere act of learning how to acknowledge yourself is important because, in order to be authentic, you must absolutely know who you are.

Authenticity takes courage. The courage comes in light of possible rejection. The courage comes from not only being able to sacrifice your comfort, but also the comfort of others. In moments of inauthenticity, we our catering to other's feelings and perspectives. We consider how others will feel or what others will think about us. We say yes when we mean no, and no when we mean yes. We accept what we don't want. We go where we don't want to go and do what we don't want to do. We cease living to satisfy the expectations of others and live according to whatever our truths may be. Who we are, or aspects of who we are may not always be understandable or sensical for others, but it does not matter because our lives are our own.

Authenticity gives way to personal freedom because you get to live life for yourself. Now, of course, if others depend on you, and you are central to the inner-workings of a dynamic outside of yourself, authenticity can feel difficult, but I believe there is always a way to embrace and express our true selves. In self-love, we can be authentic because we know that we are good enough and who we are at our core, matters. In self-love, we know the value of stepping out of the shadows that keep us from hiding ourselves from the world. We step out from the shadows of shame and discomfort, and into the light of transparency and authenticity.

Consider, if and when you are blessed to be around people that you feel safe with to be your honest self, and not hide the parts of you that you would typically hide around others. Doesn't it feel like a moment of exhaling and ease? It takes more mental energy to put on masks, to strategize how we can hide, and to filter what we honestly want to say. So to allow yourself to just "BE," which can initially seem difficult, eventually offers an experience of internal freedom.

Let's take a look at the implications of wearing masks. We are taught to put on masks in all types of settings and under various conditions to live life in a favorable way. We wear different masks around family members, friends, authority figures, "gatekeepers," romantic interests, and the general public. Wearing a mask seems more intuitive than not wearing a mask. We are taught that life is a game. We learn the realities of people's judgments, prejudices, and biases. We learn that we must look and play parts that, even though not aligned with who we truly are, provide the opportunity to get to where we want to be in life.

The notion of mask application is most prevalent for people of color in homogenous non-color spaces/societies. If one's ethnic identity is often associated with negative prejudices, a person may feel more inclined to make the majority feel comfortable by changing their appearance, speech, and mannerisms. Who they present themselves to be, can create compartmentalized identities to the point that one experiences disconnection with their true selves. You are challenged to believe that your being, which to others is connected to prejudices and stereotypes, is one-dimensionally insufficient or defective. This creates intense intrapersonal conflicts and causes one to question themselves, and even experience what has come to be called imposter syndrome. You are not able to connect to the gravity of your own success or the impact you've made because your mind has been trained to believe you are not good enough, and very little of what you do in life matters. It's an intense experience that people have, and it robs them of being able to sit in the gratitude, beauty, and miracles that have come to fruition in their life.

Being disconnected from our identities is one aspect of inauthenticity. Being disconnected from our emotions is another experience. Overuse and application of the words "fine," "good," or "ok" are prime examples of how some are inauthentic or more so, not completely honest with expressing their emotional or mental states. It's so very a part of the US American experience to ask someone how they are doing, and the most likely response is good, ok, or fine. Rarely do people admit to bad, difficult, challenging, or worrisome. Its' much more difficult for someone to honestly share that they are currently in a state of confusion, melancholy, regret, overwhelm, despair, or anger.

We have been socialized to ask how someone is doing, and have also been socialized to answer in a way that doesn't open a conversation that is "too deep," "too much for the other to handle" or "too uncomfortable." Consequentially, we learn to mask and minimize our feelings. Tucking them away and either averting them completely or sharing them with a minimal amount of people. Just as your self is important, so are your emotional experiences. The consequence of constantly minimizing and suppressing your emotions creates more intrapersonal conflict, as well as a gateway to unhealthy coping skills, ineffective communication, and shallow relationships.

As a psychotherapist, two of my main intentions are to support others in connecting to their true selves aside from their illness and to understand and communicate their emotions. Our emotions give us necessary information, but we are so disconnected from the impact that stimuli has on us, that we lack the extra insight to interpret how we really feel.

Our fear and discomfort around expressing ourselves are often connected to our perceived level of safety around vulnerability. We additionally consider what someone else would think about us and our emotional state. There are enough unsaid norms about sharing "too much" or not letting people into our inner lives, but the irony is that people feel ok sharing about transitions in their careers, family lives, and even the food they eat. Sharing how we feel is more about the general discomfort of vulnerability and fear of judgment. Because what would it mean if people actually knew the complete authentic us? We fear that they would reject us. We fear that they would ostracize us, or talk ill of us. We fear that we may lose access to being a part of something. Maybe someone told you that your feelings didn't matter. Maybe someone told you that it makes more sense to deal with your emotions on your own. Maybe you had an experience of expressing yourself, and the consequence was harassment, abuse, or belittling. Because of this experience, you made the decision that it's better to deal with your emotions on your own, or maybe it's too much of a hassle.

A step further in exploring this issue is considering what happens when we think our emotions or who we are is "too much." Someone, somewhere, at some point in your life, gave you a reason to believe you were too much.

They didn't know how to support you; they didn't know how to respond to you; they said who you are and how you present yourself was too overwhelming for them. As a result, you decided to temper down how you express and present yourself. The fear, fixation, or concern of being "too much" imprisons you above anything. The experience of feeling like you're too much leads you to walk on eggshells and to be uncomfortable with and hypersensitive of what you say and how you say it. Your body is in an alert state, just because the risk of authenticity seems like too much.

Each day you go out into the world, not only utilizing the energy you need for your school, vocation, profession, or daily duties, but many people have to use extra energy to be the person they really aren't, or to be an altered version of someone they are. Once we can surrender to authenticity, the journey of walking in self-love becomes less strenuous; it doesn't seem esoteric and elusive. It is in authenticity that we can be honest with ourselves about where we are mentally, physically, spiritually, and honestly ask for assistance or come up with help/support to help us navigate thru the five commandments of self-love. At times we think we're being honest, but far too often, we find ways to truly distract and disconnect from who we are, what we feel and the reality of what's going on within.

In light of all that helps us on our journey of self-love, it's important to note that we are constantly shifting. Our authenticity can always be challenged. *We can ask ourselves, can I share more of myself? Can I embrace more of myself?* We can always dig deeper to acknowledge and accept more. It takes a consistent re-visitation of who we really are. Authenticity takes renewal because if we are honestly growing, we are constantly transforming. What authenticity looks like for us in one season in our life, can look gravely different in another. Authenticity changes because who we are is changing, if we are living our life in a way that promotes growth and honoring our highest state of being. The ability to practice boundaries, move between various environments, cultivate different skills, be open to new experiences, all create an internal experience that represents evolution.

A challenging aspect of these so-called personal evolutions often involves others seeing you different. You don't appear the same to them, and in many ways, you may not be. Others may feel threatened by your shifts; some may feel drawn to you because of your shifts, while others' may not know what to do in relation to your ever-shifting self. No matter how people respond to you, remember that first and foremost, your self-love journey is about how you live your life. We all have one life to live, and it is important to understand we have more agency and free will than we give ourselves. You can live an empowered life. You can live an intentional life. You can live a life that allows you to honor your personal sense of freedom. You can live life having unapologetic confidence, courage, conviction, and faith. Living life unapologetically authentic, challenging norms of expression, and not being driven by validation or acceptance of others is absolutely a road less traveled. One that lives that life is an anomaly. It takes courage over and over again. The courage that I know you can have if you choose to. There have been spiritual leaders throughout our history that have shown us what a life of love, honor, and enlightenment of self can look like. It is possible, and it is available to you.

Owning Your Journey

Owning your journey is about accountability and unapologetic acceptance. Owning your journey is about awareness. Owning your journey is about accepting what has occurred in your life, and accepting how the choices you have made have impacted your life as well as others. It sounds simple, but it is anything but simple.

Behind our smiles, our titles, our accomplishments, and our relationships often lie shame and regret, shame about some aspect of ourselves. Shame around the choices we've made. Regret around what we have and haven't done. These emotional experiences keep us from accepting ourselves or aspects of our lives. The experiences surely keep one from practicing Radical Acceptance. Radical acceptance is about embracing what is, and not resisting what you cannot or choose not to change. Radical acceptance is about being in the present and getting to a place of consciousness to believe that what is, is, and what isn't, doesn't exist; if it were, it would be what is.

It is difficult for many to embrace and accept who they are because they are more fixated on who they are not. The fixation is often based on comparison. People choose to see lack within themselves because they glorify the life and decisions of others. This comparison does nothing but harms one's psyche. In a world of technology that has all types of media platforms filled with images and stories of others' lives, it's difficult for many of us to not fall into comparison. We are bombarded with images of so many ways to live. We have ushered in an industry of people getting paid to showcase the highlights of their life. We have reality TV, which is anything but reality. There are endless articles, blog posts, and books about "how to" live, be, and exist. To a degree, this is one of those books. People feel inadequate if their lives don't look like or seem aligned with the vision of life that their favorite figures and influencers portray.

How can you own your journey, when you are focused on living the journey of another? If one exists in a constant state of comparison and dissatisfaction of their own life, it may threaten one's ability to practice and harness the power of gratitude. It also blocks your ability to focus on the power you hold within to shape your own life. When you connect to the power that you hold, you foster a deeper sense of resilience, confidence, and appreciation for yourself and your life. Regardless, if you are a person that has any or no connection to the transcendental experience, there is something powerful and transformative about belief. Belief, for many, is about faith in something. If you can believe in what looks like a beautiful, affirming, and powerful unfolding in someone else's life, work on seeing your life and your being thru that same lens.

When you can cease the monster of comparison, you can truly have a sense of confidence in yourself and the unfolding of your life. After a string of events throughout the years that let left me emotionally, spiritually, and mentally drained, it seemed difficult to stand in an unapologetically grounded place of strong confidence. I found myself experiencing wavering confidence; very different from the sense of groundedness and security I used to have before these strong events occurred. When I eventually returned to myself, I had to reflect on how the confidence came to be a settled reality once again. I felt so powerful in myself and who I was; I asked myself, *where did my confidence come from?*

The answer I received from my higher self was the following:

You feel powerful because now you understand how powerful you are. Power can only be harnessed if you hold on to it. To access it, it must not be in the hands of anyone else. You can't have power over something that is not yours.

Meaning, if I give away my power to others, it could never be mine. To harness my power, I must own my own truth. I must know my own truth. I must take responsibility for what I have chosen in my life. I must accept the events that were out of my control. I must take accountability for my actions and how I have decided to navigate my life. I must release anger, bitterness, or envy that held me captive in regards to other's lives or the choices others' made that impacted me. My confidence reflects the power I know I have. The power I have is a reflection of the place of acceptance I am in my life. All in all, it is the fruit of self-love.

To accept who you are means there is a cognitive and spiritual process of understanding who you are and what has shaped you, but even that is not the same as owning who you are.

As previously mentioned in the section, "Desire for Change," the 5 stage of the model of change provides a conceptual framework of what it takes for someone to commit to change. Part of that change is not only acceptance of what has happened, but also action to move forward once you have received awareness, tools, and guidance. Change doesn't stop at an awareness or the receiving of tools and guidance. Change, shifting, transformation, and any other personal journey takes the individual's concerted effort. This is even why therapy "does not work" for many people. They enter a therapeutic relationship with their therapy professional, expecting that the therapist will "fix them" or give them the answers. They hope that the therapists will give them the insight that they need, yet often don't get that the therapist is a vessel, support, a mirror, or merely a provider of tools and resources.

Here's the greatest caveat: no one can save you, and no one can do the work for you. We may be blessed with understanding, sympathetic, and loving individuals to support, encourage, and hold us accountable, but at the end of the day, we are the masters of our own lives. It is us up to us to create an internal environment that is comfortable for us to thrive in. What goes on the outside of you means a fraction compared to what is going on within you. Your internal peace and acceptance are important in navigating this life. You are stuck with yourself. You are stuck with your own thoughts and emotions. You reap the consequences of your actions. You must be carried by your own body. Therefore, understanding your relationship to how you operate in the five commandments of self-love is important.

YOU have to do the work. YOU have to dig into your truth. YOU have to assess how much of your truth is an objective reality. YOU have to ask the questions. YOU have to seek the help. YOU have to see mental health specialists, life coaches, and specialized healers. YOU have to create or engage in opportunities for personal development and self-growth. There is no one route. It will be tough at times, and carefree at others. YOU have to build up your toolbox. YOU must find what works for you. What may work for me, or others, may not be the same for you.

There are opportunities that provide a mirror into truths that have been buried by your subconscious. Tools like books, seminars, workshops, retreats, and other special programming. However, even these avenues will not be enough to unlock all the necessary guidance and insight you need to build a better relationship with yourself. It's all up to you. So you must own the journey and absolutely understand there is no destination. The destination is defined by where you are at the place of death. Right before your eyes closed. Is there internal peace? Is there self-gratitude, appreciation, and acceptance?

Nurturing Your Inner Child

For many adults who grew up in environments that were marked by abuse, neglect, and/or criticism, there is a lingering experience of shame, guilt, and fear of failure or abandonment, which often follows them into adulthood. Author, teacher, and therapist, John Bradshaw, developed, wrote, and spoke about the concept of the "Wounded Inner Child." Many adults walk around with wounds that were developed in childhood. These wounds show up and impact their present emotional experience as an adult, and they are often unaware.

It's important for you to understand and identify what brings out you inner child so that you can learn how to interact with them, nurture, and care for them, possibly unlike the way your caregivers did. If your inner child is not wounded, then it is still important to engage with activities that keep it alive and strong. Our wounded inner child is often responsible for gravitating towards behaviors and relationships that do not serve us. Our wounded child gravitates towards behaviors and modes of expression that allow it to be seen. As children often have challenges with emotional regulation and how to properly communicate their needs due to limited vocabulary or insight, so do our adult selves when our inner child is activated. Your inner child may be the part of you that wants to run away or "act out" when you don't get your way. Your inner child may feel intense shame or guilt when your critical voice feels intensely real and loud. Your inner child may feel pressure to be perfect so that you don't disappoint another. Your inner child may be responsible for your motivation to please others or be agreeable so that you don't "make someone angry" or cause them to walk away/abandon you As intense as these cycles of psychological experiences can be for your inner child, you have the power to tame, regulate, and manage your inner child.

With awareness, you get to be the gentle, nurturing, supportive, and present caregiver that your inner child did not have. It's important to know what age you believe the wounded inner child in you is, so you can recall what traumas or challenges they were facing. *Are you able to identify the age of your wounded inner child?* When you identify the child, identify or try to recall what challenges they were experiencing at that time. *Who did your wounded inner child have strained relationships with? What are the emotions your wounded inner child often faced, and who was the catalyst for these emotions?*

As you maneuver your self-love journey and work on honoring yourself, acknowledging and being gentle with your wounded inner child is imperative because when they come to surface, you are disconnected from the truth that exists at that moment. You may retreat back to a mental and emotional state that existed years ago. One must learn at the moment to say, "You are not 4, 8, 12, etc." anymore. You must learn to tell your wounded inner child that they will be ok. If they take control of a moment or an interaction, we must also learn to be honest and recognize that we are hurt at any given moment. We can learn to accept what is going on, and possibly communicate with someone that we responded or reacted from a place of hurt, fear, etc.

How exactly can you go about nurturing your wounded inner child? Consider that a child will gage who they can trust and be comfortable with. As the main caregiver of your wounded inner child, you want to make sure, when emotions or thoughts of your wounded inner child arrive, you create an internal space of non-judgment, safety, and openness. Because your inner child is fearful, they have to feel that they can trust you. Due to fear and shame being the most pervasive emotions, validating your inner child's experience is also important. Provide words of encouragement and affirmation. Also, speak to your inner child in a way that reflects you understand why they feel the way they do. That brings me to the next point – Allow your child to feel what they feel, whether that's anger or sadness. Encourage the experience of remorse, and reframe the context for the child.

Your wounded inner child needs healing. Your wounded inner child needs gentleness. Your wounded inner child needs a safe space to be vulnerable. Your wounded inner child often feels flawed, imperfect, and deficient. Thus, to comfort them in the midst of what feels like loneliness or abandonment is your role. *What would it mean if we could take the time, to be honest, admit, and take steps to support our wounded inner child?* You may be an adult that prides themselves off of responsibility, accolade, power, influence, or leadership; however, if you have an wounded inner child, you do yourself a disservice by ignoring it. You cannot ignore your wounded inner child because that will allow the depths of the wounds to continue to expand. To continue to feel like they are not good enough or worthy enough of love, affection, respect, or care, the cycle of abuse or neglect that the wounded inner child was shaped in continues.

One can experience shame around feeling the brokenness, insecurity, or fear that comes from the activation of a wound that has power over your inner child. Shame is a dark covering of experience of authenticity and unapologetic acceptance. In order to sit, stand, or walk in the full power that self-love can bring, we must actively engage in defeating the enemies that exist within our mind and heart spaces. The enemy is often us or the narratives we take on, which has damaged us so strongly. It can feel "immature" or silly to come face to face with the notion of a child-like dimension of your being in existence, but your thought about it does not change the truth of its' existence. I'll leave you with these words by John Bradshaw, "To truly be committed to a life of honesty, love, and discipline, we must be willing to commit ourselves to reality."

The Intertwining Entities

It is important to note that everything in this universe is connected. In discussing the 5 Commandments, it's important to know that they don't just function as silos. Even when you consider the question, *how am I honoring myself, mind, body, and spirit?,* it's imperative to know that what you do to dimension, always impacts the others. Beings have the tendency to look at their mind, body, and spirit as separate entities. Even though each part serves its purpose and rules over a specific dimension of your being, each part exists as an intertwining entity of you. Your body, what you put in it and on it, how you treat it, and how you see it, affect your mind and spirit. Likewise, the state of your mind affects what occurs in your body. When the mind and spirit clash, your body is affected; whatever state your spirit is in, drives your mind and body.

Therefore, as we respect the interconnectedness of these entities, we can see that in their wholeness, they represent our whole selves, which is why the first commandment of self-love is to Honor Thyself. Honoring thyself, at the one-time moment, is you honoring the full totality of your being. It is you understanding that you are one being made of many parts, and to be able to honor yourself is collectively honoring all the intertwining entities within you.

As we move forward in the text, recognize that even though the three commandments to follow are separated into honor thy mind, honor thy body, and honor thy spirit, there will be many examinations of how they impact one another.

What if I told you that there is research that has deducted that stress can be just as harmful on your body as your diet. Stress, especially in women, changes your body's ability to ward off or develop fat cells. There have been studies in mice showing that females put under stress would experience a change in gut bacteria, which typically would fight the development of fat cells[vi].

Understanding that your mental and physical health can be influenced by emotional and spiritual states is vital as well. More and more research has shown how there is a relationship between depression and an emergent risk of death. What about your spiritual and physical health? Brain scans see that when individuals are praying or practicing some sense of gratitude, the same areas of the brain are activated as if someone was experiencing a pleasant activity.

Earlier, I discussed the background of the ACE study, where researchers saw a relationship between higher occurrences of ACES and health outcomes such as compromised mental functioning, unwanted pregnancies, STDs/STIs, cardiovascular illnesses, obesity, and diabetes.

We often look at life and our present place in it as coincidental circumstance, when in actuality, there are many intertwining factors that shaped us and impacted the position and place that we exist in. What we believe to be decisions lead by choice are often unconscious habitual patterns that we've carried because of our life experiences.

With science backing the tie between lived experiences and health, it can be understood that experiences as a child and adult affect how we function. Our experiences shape how we look at ourselves, navigate life, and even how we operate and contribute to society. We must take accountability for our beings.

Once we step into a stance of consciousness about where we are in relation to the commandments of self-love, proactiveness is important. If we are trauma survivors or individuals with a high level of stress due to our life commitments, choosing to acknowledge where we are and what we can do to improve or manage our wellbeing is an advisable step. In honoring ourselves, we are giving voice to where we are at any moment in time and in any season of life and doing what we need to do to make sure we are thriving.

Societal change may help explain the emergent risk of death for women with depression.

"During the last 20 years of the study in which women's risk of death increased significantly, roles have changed dramatically both at home and in the workplace, and many women shoulder multiple responsibilities and expectations," says Dr. Colman

Stepping Into Knowing Yourself

Who am I? What is my identity? Who am I in my eyes? Who am I to the world?

What does it mean to "know" yourself?

As I maneuvered my 20s, every year, I would sit in reflection before my birthday and take in all the lessons from the previous and assessing my growth. Typically, I would get to the point of saying, wow, I've experienced a lot, and I'm glad I know myself. Ha...then the next year, I would realize, wow, I grew more and more. The point is that I believe there is only one point in time, where we can make a full assessment about who we are, and that is within our last breaths — any time before that is rather premature. Every second, day, week, month, year, and decade brings new lessons and opportunities for us to grow. So whoever you are in this moment, will not exactly be the same in months or years from now.

At every point, we are a collection of our experiences and exposures. We are a reflection of what we are watching, reading, listening to, and digesting. Everything that stimulates us affects our minds and our behavior. Whatever you feed your mind shapes your thoughts; your thoughts shape your perception of yourself as well as your perception of the world; your perception shapes your beliefs; your beliefs shape your habits and habits become the root of your actions. Your life then becomes a reflection of the actions that you did or did not take.

It all matters.

Coming to know yourself is unequivocally a life long journey, however, stepping into knowing yourself, is an easier and more intentional task. Within the notion of honoring yourself, stepping into knowing your self would be best defined as the active assessment of what shapes and motivates you.

When you go to any type of physician, in order to gain a perspective on who you are, what you need, and how they can serve you, they have an intake and assessment process. They ask you questions about your family history, your current living conditions, your schedule, habits, etc. They are assessing the status of your health based on a collection of information, and are not just relying on the information you willingly decide to offer them. Why is that? Well, in general, whatever we perceive to be the truth is often just a fraction of it. There's almost always a deeper underlying reason for our perceptions. There are underlying reasons why we choose our friends, our network, our home, our jobs, our partners, and all the details of our lives day today. Nothing really "just happens." The medical professional knows that you just don't get sick, for the heck of it. Your body is responding, fighting, or protecting itself because of a trauma, imbalance, unhealthy intruder, or a mutation.

Therefore, in stepping into knowing ourselves, we must learn to ask the questions that help us understand why we do, act, feel, and think the way we do. *What is motivating us? Are we acting, reacting, or staying still because of fear or love? What makes us stay in a box or step out of it? What pushes us past a boundary? What keeps us within a boundary? Why do we behave the way we do in our relationships? Why do we surrender or stand in our power? Why do we feel insecure? Why do we feel confident? Why are we confused? How do we know we trust ourselves? What triggers us? What contributes to our comfort? What are our boundaries? When do we go beyond them? When do we allow others to cross them? How do we define joy? How do we define happiness? How do we define success? What unhealthy behaviors do we hold on to? What limited thoughts do we hold on to?*

I challenge you to create a physical space to reflect on these questions. The physical space could be a journal, your phone, an art canvas, or any other medium that allows you to capture your thoughts and emotions.

You are multifaceted. You are complex. You are unique. Most importantly, you are human. You've made decisions that would have been different, had you more wisdom. You've allowed people to stay in your life past their expiration date. You've stayed in environments and relationships past their expiration date. Sometimes, you make leaps and bounds, and other times, you're fearful of taking a small step. Sometimes, you communicate clearly and other times, you don't know what to say. Sometimes, you can handle all that life throws at you, while other times, you want to throw your hands up. You are imperfectly perfect, and it's important to give yourself the space to be all the people you can be, without judgment. Dare I repeat, without judgment.

Judgment is the challenging barrier that keeps us from embracing and accepting who we are. Thru the lens judgment, falling isn't just falling. With an eye of judgment, falling is bad, and you fell because you're a bad, inadequate, lazy, or uncoordinated person. Thru judgment, we can't accept an act as an act; we must (according to our egos function) assign any thought or behavior as bad or good. When we say we are not enough, it's because we are bad. When we praise ourselves, it's because we are good?

In stepping into knowing yourself and in efforts to learning to accept yourself, the goal is just about understanding. Having the awareness to ask the question why, and having the ability, discernment, and introspection to answer the question.

Commandment 2: Honor Thy Mind

Process of Socialization

I believe that we are in a time where social consciousness has increasingly deepened around the impact of systems, institutions, and beliefs that shape our socialization. Socialization references the process of impacting how an individual learns to integrate into their society. It encompasses the structures of a working society that allows an individual to develop an understanding of how the world around them works and how they can be apart of it. There are parts of us that are intuitive and natural, and there are other aspects of us that are gravely shaped by circumstances around our birth (location, decade, family, and birth order), the geographic location we are raised, institutions we are connected to, like schools and religion, media, and political infrastructures.

For many years, the socialization process has been something that social scientists have focused on. Social scientists have engaged in research on what tools societies have used to socialize their citizens. Within recent years, an increasing number of individuals are seeking out resources and information that exposes them to information that has often been shared in communities of academia or influence. People are practicing the power of critically and theoretically approaching what drives human social, emotional, physical, and political experience. People raise questions that challenge previously accepted norms. People are more apt to have dialogue and pose questions that explore, *"what is the purpose of life? What motivates and shapes my behavior? What motivates and shapes others' behaviors? What makes people different or similar? What are the patterns of behaviors that exist, and how do I/we go about changing those behaviors?*

With the wealth of information available in print and online media, individuals are actually becoming social scientists outside of an academic setting. There are many ways that the exchange of information exists. Blogging, social media, vlogging, and the use of memes have been major avenues for individuals to disseminate information. It is more common nowadays for individuals to question what's considered "normal" than to accept life for the way it is. People constantly challenge the constructions that we have around different aspects of our identity, such as ethnicity, gender, gender roles, sexuality, and various social roles. There is a consistent challenge of political systems, leadership, and practices. People challenge the invisibility of intersection. When we look at the process of socialization, we must realize how finely intricate everything is.

Every single interaction influences us. Every single person that takes care of us influences us. Every device we use. The ideologies that we believe in, which impact how we think, act, speak, or treat someone else, are part of our socialization process. We like to confine or simplify the reasonings of what makes people who they are. We look at astrology. We look to numerology. We look to the spirit realm. We look to the environment. We look to ethnicity. We look to culture. There are many systems and concepts that we use in our attempt to analyze or understand others' behavior and disposition. Humans are not simple creatures; therefore, oversimplifying what contributes to the shaping of someone only does injustice to the complexity of the many contributing factors.

Whatever the contributing factors have been, if one wants to be able to more efficiently manage how they show up in the world or understand why they experience the type of relationship they do with themselves, it's important to consider these questions: *what thoughts are produced in my mind? What are the natures of my thoughts? What is shaping my thoughts?* Everything that you believe in shapes how you see and relationship with yourself. We must always examine the quality of our thoughts because they often are the tint on the lens that we use to look at the world.

Audio stimulation & Visual stimulation

How mindful are you of what you listen to or watch? Considering that sounds and images are all around us and that we are inundated with millions of sounds and images a day, it's important to consider how these sounds and images can impact us. According to Oxford, sound is vibrations that travel thru the air or another medium and can be heard when they reach a person's or animal's ear. In psychology, sound is the reception of such audible mechanical waves and their perception by the brain. It's important to note that like vibrations, sound is energy. Energy in any form is transferrable. It can neither be created nor destroyed. So in understanding that a sound is a form of energy, consider that sound is transferable energy that can have an impact on your mind.

There are many sounds that we are not conscious of, which can impact our mood. However, there are many sounds that we can be mindful and selective in the process of our interaction. The language that others use and what you listen to, is important to be mindful of. Words have power. They can be spoked to empower or degrade. Words can be spoken to enrich and teach, or tear down and poison. On a day to day basis, we may listen to music or watch music/video. With social media as a central aspect of socializing nowadays, there are millions of videos that are posted daily. Major articles often include sound bites of major events that are being covered.

If you are listening to or watching anything that is not providing affirmative, nurturing, or positively informative content, you could very well be exposing yourself to energy that does not allow you to honor yourself. Our main media sources push to share the news that reports about the pain, hurt, struggle, violence, and negativity going on around us. The resulting emotions from these stories can result in anger, frustration, invisibility, sorrow, depression, sadness, fear, and hopelessness. It seems for every ten stories of warning; there may be one sharing about a good deed that has occurred. We also experience segments that focus on what we can buy to "make our lives better." We hear about celebrity gossip and become entangled in the lives of others. There are often segments based on how to "diet

119

better" and "lose weight," which continues to feed the diet culture that exists. Outside of just your daily news bits, there is so much that you audibly ingest that creates an internal experience of low-frequency emotions.

Persistent exposure to such stories, especially on a daily basis, impacts how we see the world, and our ability to be safe in it. Not only do these stories impact how we see the world, but it impacts how we see our communities, our families, and ourselves.

Consider if you're someone with body image issues, you wake up feeling content with yourself, and then you hear or see a diet ad? More than likely, this will ignite your insecurity, and you will be more prone to think about how much you should or should not eat during the day; you may fixate on the parts of your body you're not pleased with. What you hear shapes your thoughts. If you are not selective with what you listen to, you are less aware of the source of your thoughts.

Sometimes, people listen and watch content before going to sleep, wondering why they may have difficulty falling asleep, sleeping peacefully, or waking in peace. The content you take in or may take leaves residue on your thoughts. If you listen or watch something with language that does not promote peace, serenity, or relaxation, it would be no surprise as to why you would have an experience that may represent the opposite.

Self-talk

The sentence that begins with the words I am is powerful, but even more impactful are the words that follow. The words you declare to be your truth, or define who you are, shape your own self-perception. How you see yourself, in turn, makes an impact on how you speak to yourself.

In considering how you speak to yourself – Are you encouraging? Affirming? Critical? Over-critical? Judgmental? Gentle? Harsh?

Do you speak to others as you speak to yourself, whether in your best or worst moments? Do others speak to you how you speak to yourself in your best or worst moments?

I would like to raise a bigger question: Are you completely conscious of how you speak to yourself at all times? Chances are that there are times when you speak of limitation. Do any of the following phrases come to mind? I can't, you are not, you don't deserve, you can't, you are not "X" enough, you're not ready, you're too "X" to do that, etc. Let's be honest. Even the most confident person around has moments of insecurity. It happens. It's not the fleeting moments of doubt that imprison us. It's the reoccurring script that we play that affects us most.

As mentioned earlier, we must remember that our thoughts affect our actions; our behavior shapes our habits, our shape, our lives. When we consider where we are in our life, it's advantageous to consider what our thought patterns have been like, as well as what specifically do we say to ourselves at our best, worse, and in between. Do we coach ourselves to greatness and remember that life is like a game, you win some, and you lose some. Or do we speak to ourselves like Cinderella's wicked step-mother, making sure we stay in the place of limitation that we've decided to place yourself?

Self-talk isn't just about what you murmur or say aloud to yourself. It also matters the thoughts that you are ruminating on. Self-talk was possibly and still is possibly one of the most challenging areas for me. The reality is, we will think negative thoughts about life, and we will, at times, think negative thoughts about ourselves. For me, as for many others, the critical voice can be so loud. The critical voice is the voice lingering from one's dissatisfied ego. It is the voice that won't accept the reality of a circumstance and instead decides to heighten worry, anxiety, and dissatisfaction. Critique has its place when it comes to a focus on elevation, improvement, and growth. Otherwise, it can be a rather dangerous habit and mechanism of our minds.

There is a fine line between what we perceive to be self-growth and personal development versus self-critique and dangerous criticism. On the journey of pursuing our next level, we can become so hard on ourselves for where we currently are. Asking questions like, *how did I get here? What is the mindset that I have that is shaping my current state?* These are healthy introspective questions, but sometimes that critical voice can get loud and lead you to questions like, why am I not smarter? Why am I not like him or her? Why am I not good enough? We ask questions of judgment and answer them with even harsher criticism and judgment.

We attack who we are. We attack our values. We attack how we look. We attack and criticize ourselves because we're not living up to or we don't see ourselves living up to some constructed standard that has been projected on our psyches thru media, relationships, or comparison. You may have family that has passed down ideas of who you "should" be, how you "should" behave, how you "should" look, and how your life "should" turn out. This pressure, these ideas, and this information gathered from all these sources becomes the power igniting fluid for the fire of self-criticism that resides in you. It can be really hard to actually quiet that voice. What I've learned is sometimes when you hear it, the best you can do is step outside of yourself and tell the voice to be quiet. You learn to step outside of yourself and acknowledge that the voice is incorrect and challenge it. You challenge it with an affirmation. You challenge it by stating truthful counter-evidence to yourself. You challenge it by simply re-framing what the thought was.

The most important technique to facing the critical voice is by being aware of it. For some of us, such as myself, the voice can react so swiftly when making decisions; you may not even realize it. I have learned to actively step out of myself so that I can speak truth and gentleness into my consciousness. At the end of the day, the loudest and harshest of critical voices are based on fear, irrationality, and an unrealistic world of perfection. These voices are quick to speak of your faults and slow to acknowledge your successes. For someone that is goal-oriented, your critical voice can lead you down a road of overly exerted efforts and a complicated discontent for life. Constantly chasing perfection is both exhausting and mentally debilitating. Those who have an intense ability to be over self-critical, typically score lower on indexes measuring happiness and overall satisfaction in life.

You must treat your critical voice as a mischievous child. You can learn how to nurture the voice. You can be gentle. You can be mindful of grounding phrases. You can be intentional about challenging your own thoughts. You can journal about your criticism, to capture on paper the lies or harshness you say to yourself, and learn how to replace such statements. You can challenge yourself to speak to yourself as if you were someone you admired or cared about. Positive self- talk is difficult when one is socialized always to pick out faults and errors; therefore, it takes intentional, conscious efforts to learn how to do it.

Seeds from the Garden of Others

One of the greatest lies ever told was, "stick and stones may break my bones, but words will never hurt me." This line from the famous child's rhyme has the wonderful intention of providing encouragement and a sense of power to a child who is the target of bullying or name-calling. It's supposed to be a call to ignore the taunting, and to walk away with pride, knowing that what another child says doesn't matter. That's beautiful, idealistic, and oversimplified for a child to really comprehend. It's oversimplified because it doesn't truly speak to why not taking what others say personally or absorbing what others do and say matters. It also does not give a child space to understand the emotional experience they have, should someone call them a name, or make fun of them.

In reflecting on the application of this rhyme, there are two very real realities that stick out: adults could learn from that song, but also, as humans, we are connected to one another, so the truth is, what we do and say, does impact each other. The most spiritually evolved and enlightened people amongst us can speak to the power of not being impacted by others; however, words have power, and the average person feels them. Any religion, ancient wisdom, or spiritual teachings, speaks to the power that words have in shaping our reality and impacting our emotional beings. Words have the weight to empower and invigorate, or weaken and destroy.

When individuals speak of abuse, they often think of and focus on physical abuse; they, however, fail to really talk about the detrimental effects of the other forms of abuse, such as financial, psychological, and verbal abuse. Verbal abuse is the use of belittling, demeaning, and demoralizing words, often coupled with criticism towards another for the sake of maintaining a sense of power and control. There are many people who were raised in verbally abusive homes or have been in relationships that consist of verbal abuse.

For the average person who carries some form of insecurity, verbal abuse, or dishonoring words can be really challenging to listen to. It takes someone with thick skin, emotional disconnection, or a strong sense of self not to be dramatically impacted by the words others use. Verbal abuse and criticism can be just as emotionally and psychologically damaging as the experience of physical abuse. In such an environment, you are developing a narrative that you are not safe, not loved, not loveable, not worthy, not accepted, not enough, or are problematic. One can experience the remnants of trauma, whether being exposed to physical or verbal abuse.

It's the words that people say that often motivate others to be their best selves, or creates the reasons for people to give up or release their dreams. Far too often, someone somewhere tells a dreaming, hard-working, and ambitious person, that they can't make whatever goal they are working towards or are hoping to achieve. The words of doubt can either be the steam to propel someone forward to accomplish what another said they couldn't, or those words can burn thru someone's soul, destroying any motivation that existed.

It may be the case that words from some sources impact you less than words from others. It is important to learn to stay anchored and grounded in yourself when others speak incorrectly, ill, or small of you; however, it's often easier said than done. Projection from others can fuel the fire for a life narrative that promotes self-doubt, confusion, and disarray. This is why it's important that you are not only mindful of the words you speak to yourself, but also the people you surround yourself with, and the way they speak to you. Every word that you hear is like a seed. It's up to you to decide what happens with those seeds; whether you water and nurture them, or leave on barren ground, so that they stay as seeds, and never bear fruit.

People are often careless with words because people are often not aware of what they are saying or its impact. I find that one, who is more intentional and impeccable with their words, will be able to see how much variation exists when it comes to this. Consider your spirit like a garden, a garden full of flora, plants, and trees. For a garden to flourish, it needs to be tended to. The flowers, plants, and trees need nutrients in the soil and above ground in the form of water. They need sunlight. They need to be tended to. Not only is it about how you tend to them, but they are impacted by bees, pollination, and other insects. There is a lot that can go on in a garden. Be sure to speak life. Be sure to speak the truth and challenge the seeds that poison or tarnish your garden.

Commandment 3: Honor Thy Body

The Complexity of Honoring the Body

The body is often the primary gateway to someone being able to gauge their esteem, acceptance, and relationships with themselves. Honoring the body takes place in so many ways; it's a bit more complicated than the other commandments. In honoring the body, it serves us to keep in mind what we put on our body, as well as what we put in our body. It is just as important to be mindful of how environments and exposure to various elements, such as words and actions. Because our bodies are the houses of our spirit, it's important to know what our body experiences also impacts our spirit and minds.

So much of our life is lived with little to no consciousness of how the outside world impacts our internal experience. It is not uncommon that one becomes of age and arrives at a place of awareness and consciousness; extensive healing must take place. In stages of enlightenment, you are awakened to different levels of understanding, and it takes time and much effort to unlearn what you have previously been taught and directed to believe. We learn ideas, concepts, and social norms that can be poisonous to our mind, body, and spirit. Much of what we learn shapes our relationship with our body. It would be lovely just to live and not have a complicated experience around our body, but it is often the primary representation of who we are to others and sometimes ourselves. There are constant messages being sent out about what is an acceptable and unacceptable body. There are social constructs that regulate the use of a body, and implore politics around the appropriateness of exposure and various functions.

In many ways, one can see the oppression of the body across various cultures. Doctrine controls the appropriateness of sex and physical affection. Doctrine and law control the amount of body that can be exposed. Laws control or filter the ways in which someone can use their body as capital in exchange for goods, or how to treat it at death. We have corporations that create and regulate chemicals that impact the body. Bodies are abused for pleasure and punishment. Rights and opportunities are withheld from some persons because of the way their bodies look. Limitations are put on people because of body size, ability, and color. Some bodies are even at risk because of their environment or what they look like.

Experiences that arise from trauma, oppression, harassment discrimination based on appearance, are examples of major experiences the body needs to heal from.

I am a vessel of divine power. I am a healer. I am a life enhancement specialist. I am an author and speaker. I am a survivor of complex trauma; I am a carrier of intergenerational trauma. I am a survivor of sexual assault, domestic violence, mental illness, body shaming, and colorism. I know about body-based trauma from lived experience. On my journey, I've learned to befriend the fear and anxiety I experience and decode what it is telling me. I've learned that as personal as I've taken others' criticism about my physical appearance in weight, height, complexion, build, or hair texture, I am me, and that's perfectly fine. I've learned that I am not going to fit many standards of beauty, but I am me. I've learned that my body holds on to all emotions; therefore, if I want to feel my best, I must be mindful of releasing and negative emotions that I'm holding onto.

Not only does my body hold on to emotions, but so does yours. In many cultures, people are socialized to contain and not express their emotions. Sometimes, individuals are even taught to ignore their feelings. However, I will explore the "hidden body," and how much of our emotional experience impacts our physical health.

With statistics estimating that in the US ¼ girls are sexually assaulted,1/3 women are sexually assaulted, and 1/3 adults experience a mental illness symptom in their lifetime, it is safe to say that if we looked at the emotional experience of individuals impacted by such events, we could see trends in health and life outcomes. This is exactly what brought the CDC and Kaiser to facilitate their ACE study, which was discussed earlier.

We survivors often have the habit of wanting to protect our offenders. We don't want anyone to see them as offenders, or we don't want to humiliate them. I don't believe anyone should be humiliated, but I also believe as a survivor of any trauma, there is healing in acknowledgment. The choice someone makes doesn't make them bad. It just reveals some possibly unhealthy ideologies and idiosyncrasies they may hold. One must ask, why is protecting someone else's pain or discomfort more of a priority than my own wholeness and healing?

Healing is an ACTION-LEAD process. Healing is not just about time. Healing is about forgiveness. Healing is about releasing that which has wounded you. It's about acknowledgment. It's about engulfing yourself in

132

practices and activities that bring forth awareness and restoration. Healing is also about accountability. If you feel like you have been wronged, you will not be healed if you purely victimize yourself. You must understand hurt people, hurt people. You must also understand that if you are a survivor of childhood trauma, as an adult, you have the CHOICE of what relationships you create, build, maintain, or close, especially once you become aware of the cycles and patterns that have held you captive.

I got to this moment of time in front of you because I have had an emotional and mental block for some time, during the writing process of this book. I am a writer; however, writing this section of the book has possibly offered the most difficulty. I write for myself, and I write for healing purposes for others. Writing is something I've connected to on a very spiritual level since I really engaged on my personal self-love journey. It's a spiritual practice for me. I began working on this book in 2016, and it will be published in 2019. Out of the 5 Commandments of self-love, Honor Thy Body presented to be the greatest challenge to complete.

Thru the process of developing the content for this section, I allowed myself to surrender to the greater truths that were to be revealed for both the book and my personal enlightenment. You cannot rush expansion and transformation. I have recognized that as a healer, it takes a required submission and awareness to the powers beyond me to show me the truths that deepen my wholeness and healing. The result looked like ebbs and flow of stagnation, breakdown, and breakthrough.

What I learned is that the body is often the clearest gateway into disconnection from. The basis for our understanding of safety and security is transmitted thru the body. As infants, the physical affection we're shown by caregivers impacts our connections to others. We use our little bodies to communicate our needs and wait for our caregivers to respond. We receive both feedback and criticism about our bodies, even from a young age. 1 in 5 children experiences sexual abuse, leaving emotional and mental scars for a lifetime. Children exploring their bodies can lead to healthy or rather unhealthy relationships with themselves. Adolescents exploring sexuality due to puberty and increasing peer interests, likewise, can lead to unhealthy perceptions of sexual connection, especially if a lack of information is involved. Exposure to hypersexualized images in the media leads children, adolescents, and young adults into pressure to fit ideals formulated for entertainment.

The body is often the gateway that leads one to compare the self with others and develop low esteem. The body is often the gateway that welcomes a young person to manipulate their food and body to gain validation or feel worthy of connection or attention in their family and food group. The body is often the gateway that leads to a sense of pride and confidence or shame and dissatisfaction with one's self.

When I realized, how much of my self-love journey was impacted by the wounds that were left behind because of body-related pains, it made sense that it would be the most difficult section to complete; as I had to continue healing my wounds, to come into clarity around what "honor thy body" could really mean.

My whole life, I've been on a search to understand human behavior, be an advocate, and a healer. At 8, I made up in my mind that I would be a child psychologist because "my family was crazy, and I wanted to help other kids who may have crazy families too." I got to my dream career. I become the vessel of healing I always hoped for. I've accomplished a lot academically and professionally. I have had beautiful life experiences. Over years, I realized, I could honestly say I loved my life and those in it, but I always found that there were very deep wounds that existed. There was still feelings and thoughts of inadequacy and shame, that would persists. Even as I embarked on my self-love journey on the heels of a relationship completing its purpose, I consistently knew there was a reason to go deeper for myself. Thru my self-love journey, I continued to grow in clarity around who I am, my purpose, my passion, and the desires of my life. Yet, despite my constant growth, there would always be some cosmic growth event, which would remind me that I am a trauma survivor, and it was important to continue to release what was imprisoning me. I often found that these cosmic teachers and mirrors were related to men and my body.

Years ago, I can recall a conversation with a peer who made comments about women in both a spirit of comedy and seriousness that enraged me. I mean, enraged! For me, my response was out of character. Out of his mouth, all I heard was body shaming of women and the comparison of women from various ethnic backgrounds. The anger I felt was an indication that there was something to explore. I knew then, as well as today that our emotions provide data. So I had to ask myself, even though I know he means no harm, why am I getting upset?

I was angry. I ended up journaling so much because of this interaction. In journaling, I asked myself questions and explored the layers of my emotive experience. I wrote whatever came to my spirit, and I realized one very powerful and disheartening truth: I had a fear of men. More so, I had a fear of Black men. Not a fear that impacts physical safety, but one that reflects not feeling emotionally safe. The reason I say Black men is because that is who I primarily interacted with and was impacted by. When the words hit paper, I was in shock. I was disappointed, and I was also liberated. I wrote a pure, unfiltered reflection of my truth at the time, and knew it was powerful for my healing.

I had to explore this because it cognitively didn't make sense. I would consider myself a lover. Not just from the standpoint of being a romantic person, but I am a lover of people. I am a carefree and optimistic person who has really always seen the best in people. With all that, I wondered, how could such a truth be released from my spirit?

So, in my pen, thru my pen, I allowed my spirit to speak the truth. I reflected on what the interaction with that friend meant to me, what it represented. I went down a rabbit hole of reflection, thinking about different circumstances and interactions throughout my life with key male figures, which elicited similar emotions. My friend, the one that made me so angry, represented in the moment of our interaction, every man I ever felt unsafe with or judged by. The perpetrators of colorism, the divisiveness of women, objectification, abuse, neglect, and body shaming that I didn't even know I held resentment against. He represented one of the blocks in why I could not write about Honoring My Body. He represented the trauma caused to and brought on by my body; my body in its existence and my body as a woman.

With that said, as a survivor of complex trauma, withstanding physical, emotional, verbal, psychological, and sexual abuse, often at the hands of men, it has become clear from the point of reflection and years to pass, why I had a compromised sense of safety with men. The men closest to me, within my family, those who I've dated, and some friends, are those I identify as my perpetrators. They contributed to this fear in different ways and some way more than others. It's not about pointing the finger; it's about honoring what I've experienced that had and has shaped me. In your self-love journey, part of the journey is about honoring where you are and paying attention to people, places, and events that activate wounds within you and be able to release stories told because of other people's actions or words.

It is the trauma that I had experienced and witnessed that made me so sensitive to men making demands of women. It is my trauma that shaped my disdain to speak

138

on skin color preferences of women or pit different ethnicities of women against each other. It is my trauma that ignited and sometimes still ignites, a sense of fear when I have walked passed groups of men. It is my trauma that triggers fear of being uncomfortable being around men alone. My body was in danger. My body was not honored. My body felt controlled. My body felt objectified. So as a result, I felt unsafe. Unsafe to the point I had blocks. Blocks of feeling like my best free self.

As I continuously worked on uncovering beliefs, releasing narratives, practicing forgiveness, extending compassion, and owning my own power, my relationship with my body continuously evolved, and I really got to a point where I could say, I honor my body. Honor your body because of what it has endured, and where it has brought you to. Honor your body because it is your home during your Earthly. Explore the ways that you already honor your body, and continue those practices. Explore all the ways that you do not honor your body, release what needs to be released, and continue to gather practices and rituals that will allow you to honor your body. Honoring your body is not about just the physical. As our bodies are very connected to our emotional experience, honoring the body is also about being mindful of the emotions you hold on to. Let's explore in the pages to follow.

The Hidden Body

Within our bodies lie intricate systems of cells, nerves, vessels, organs, and bones. Every aspect of our physiology serves a purpose and supports our overall well-being. Our bodies are built to function without our conscious efforts. The intricacy is complex, and this is why understanding how healing in the body isn't as simple as having a selective diet. When it comes to our relationships with our bodies, and what "healthy" looks like, a western lens would often emphasize diet, movement, and possibly self-perception. However, our bodies and what occurs within them is a reflection of so much more. There is often a misunderstanding that health can be determined by looking at someone. Sure, there are many outward manifestations of what's going on inside, but there is so much more that you don't see, and that your eyes would deceive you into believing.

I want to explore the facets of the "Hidden Body;" the part of you that cannot be seen, but is also a consistent part of your health and well-being. When we speak of Honoring Thy Body, it's important to understand the complexity of your body, and how you can build a positive and intuitive relationship with it. When you are in-tuned with your body, you can be aware of what the hidden body is telling you. Everybody has a state of homeostasis, or baseline functioning/ balance. When our bodies fall below or rise above that homeostasis, there are indicators that we can feel or see if we are alert and aware.

In efforts of exploring the hidden body, it's also important to note that one of the greatest impacts of what homeostasis looks like for one person versus another, is not only impacted by basic biology and lifestyle, but largely by their "Emotional Body" and the experiences they have lived thru, or been subjected thru DNA. The body holds on to all emotional experiences, in memory, in a narrative, and in cellular reproduction. Any experience of trauma, whether by direct impact or thru observation, vicarious, or second-hand exposure impacts your body. So to Honor Your Body means also to be connected to the experiences within your emotional body and be intentional with how you nurture and show gentleness to your emotional body.

As you may know, it's often very dramatic changes that lead someone to question if everything is ok. Once dramatic changes occur, people seek medical advice or begin to research and self-diagnose. Imagine if you didn't have to wait until it was too late? What if you knew the impact that shame, anger, guilt, sadness, loneliness, or disappointment had on your body?

There are many Indigenous, Eastern, and African healing modalities that look to focusing on the intangible, metaphysical aspects of one's being, like emotions and spirituality as indicators of health. One of the many major strengths of Eastern medicine is the focus on balancing the energy in the body due to unsettled emotions. When one engages in the ancient practice of acupuncture or takes Chinese herbs, you can receive healing treatment or interventions based on emotional experiences, as opposed to strictly going in and sharing physical symptoms, as one would do with a Western-trained physician. Eastern medicine is built around the understanding that our body's physical states reflect the flow or stagnation of energy in our bodies. The flow or stagnation of energy is often a direct reflection of our emotional and spiritual experiences. So yes, you may be experiencing irritable bowel syndrome or having intense lower back pain. However, this may be a reflection of shame or anger that you can be carrying. Emotions affect energy flow, which translates to blood flow. Life is reflective of blood flow and oxygen; when stagnation or blockage of either of these exists, dysfunction or imbalance within our various body systems and organs occur, thus, manifesting in physical ailments.

Consider the various systems that exist within our bodies: endocrine, circulatory, nervous, immune, reproductive, respiratory, and digestive systems, to name a few. Each of these systems is operating in its own capacity but is connected to and impacted by the others. All in all, each system is operating to its current capacity because of what the brain is telling it to do. When it comes to our emotions, the brain also has very specific instructions that it sends to each of these systems. When we experience different emotions, each experience releases hormones, which in turn, impact every other system.

Are you able to notice or feel what happens when you are angry? It's possible that your heart beats faster, and you become more alert. That's what you immediately feel, but there are other activities going on like your "fight or flight" system being activated, stress hormones such as cortisol and adrenaline are released, your blood vessels tighten, blood pressure increases, and your urine and bowel system temporarily shuts down. Because your body is wired to prepare to protect itself and ensure survival, your systems are prepped with what they need so you can be ready to fight or flee. If anger is a frequent emotion, this physiological response could have lasting impacts on the heart and arteries; thus, increasing your chance of heart attacks, heart disease, or other cardiovascular issues.

Anger is one of many emotions that we have the capacity to experience. In the 1970s, psychologist Paul Eckman posed a theory for six basic emotions, which are: happiness, sadness, disgust, fear, surprise, and anger. Most of our emotional experiences build-up of these. Since the 70s, research has shown, we experience emotions on a spectrum, and even some schools of thought believe we have 27 dimensions of emotions. One fact that all psychologists can agree upon is that there is a connection between emotions and physiology.

As someone looking to increase the capacity in which acceptance, compassion, celebration, and nurturing is practiced towards the self, it's important to know that your emotional experience matters. It's important to know that honoring your body includes, honoring your emotions. It's important to be aware of the mind and body connection, so if you are feeling uncomfortably nervous or cautious about something or someone, you learn to trust that your upset stomach or headache is not at "random" or coincidence. It's important to know that if you find yourself constantly feeling anxious around a person or in an environment, you take heed to that and either question why? Or explore the nature of the relationship. The constant state of anxiety may be an indicator that you may be in an unhealthy or unsafe relationship or environment, or that it may be necessary for you to explore if you can change your narrative or perception in relation to the person or environment (if it isn't unhealthy or unsafe).

Far too often, we ignore or minimize the experiences of our hidden body, not even knowing that it is giving us information that's important for our well-being I love the notion that "Emotions are data, not directives." Our emotions are valid because they are being experienced for a reason; however, there are so many factors that impact our emotional experiences, such as our perception and previous experience. We can sometimes have an emotional response based on past circumstances or emotional symbolism, as opposed to an objective connection to the stimulus. For example, it may be more natural for someone to respond with fear or anxiety to a large spider, as opposed to responding the same way if a burger was put on a plate in front of them. Both experiences are valid; however, there may be more of a psychological context as to why someone may respond in such a way with food in front of them.

When we can become more in-tuned with our Hidden Bodies, we can be more intentional with what we expose ourselves too. We can learn to honor ourselves thru intentional nurturing and care. For example, I know that I am hypersensitive to others' pain; therefore, I try to avoid movies, shows, and documentaries that profile torture, violence, or coercion of any time. Even if movies are for entertainment, I am aware that my hidden body does not know the difference, and my emotional body can become just as activated seeing a child or woman in a movie being abused, as it would if I saw someone on the street. This is also the reason why most videos that have gone viral of acts of harm and brutality have not been seen by me.

Honoring the body is being mindful of the content that triggers certain emotions, whether pleasant, neutral, or unpleasant. Just as mentioned above, your emotions trigger physiological responses; therefore, it's important to note that even if its stimuli that you read, listen to, or watch, whether real or fiction, your body will still respond accordingly. You can overstimulate your body with certain emotional experiences, and that can have long term effects.

Going back to the example I used about being mindful of taking in content with violence; research has shown, that on average, we are more desensitized to suffering because we are constantly inundated with images of violence. Our sensory systems have been rushed with so many stimuli portraying violence or harm to another person, that when most people see such content, it doesn't have such a lasting effect on them. Inversely, for some people, consistent exposure may make someone hyperaware and hypersensitive to the dangers of the world. Our brain learns how to decode and store information; this impacts what we perceive as a threat, harm, help, and everything in between.

Healing from Body-Based Trauma

Your body holds on to everything. Let me be more specific. Your body holds on to information that provides stimulating emotional experiences. Stimulating emotional experiences can be perceived as positive or negative. This is why the emotions that arise when we interact with others gives us more information than the actual behaviors themselves. Our body holds on to joy, sadness, anger, jealousy, fear, and shame. Our body also knows what "safe" feels like, and that's why environments or people can both provide that same experience. Our bodies hold on to pleasant experiences, as well as those that cause trauma and stress.

In the previous section, we explored the Hidden Body, and I shared information about what happens physiologically when we experience different emotions. In knowing that our bodies have specific physiological responses, it's important to know when those physiological responses are matched with intense emotions, especially during key stages of psychological development, or for extended periods of time, not only do markers of our health shift, but the state of our biology can change.

For the developing brain, infancy to age 4 is possibly the most pivotal when it comes to a child's understanding of safety in the world. Though a child's cognitive abilities are fairly limited, a child is ruled by their emotional body. As they cry with hopes of a caregiver meeting their needs and soothing their distress, they begin to develop a narrative of how important their needs are. They also develop a narrative as to whether they are safe enough to depend on others. Lifelong narratives begin to form, not only in regards to the relationship with their caregivers but also about their sense of safety or autonomy in the world.

The body is hypersensitivity to the world begins in the womb. Research suggests that fetuses' are impacted by the child-bearers' movements, as well as sounds that surround the child bearer's body. People like to talk to or okay music for their growing fetus because they know and believe this information to be true. What we don't talk about is what happens when there are unpleasant noises. What if the child-bearer is in an environment, or constantly interacts with someone where aggressive yelling words are constantly exchanged? That impacts the fetus as well.

After birth, the sensitivity continues as the infant's brain is developing. If there is violence or any aggressive behaviors, whether verbal or physical, those also impact the baby. It creates an experience of emotional instability and can bring force internal experiences of fear, worry, and alertness within the infant. The infant does not know what safety looks like, however may have a scarred relationship with what safety does not look like. If being exposed to violence or abuse is something that becomes normalized over time, it creates a baseline experience for the child. Children who are often exposed to violence or abuse at a very tender age are more likely to become perpetrators or victims of violence or abuse. These experiences leave imprints on the brains and literally cause change on a cellular level. They may have higher tolerances of pain, because of the desensitization that occurs, or can be extremely sensitive to any stimuli that have any remnants of the violence or abuse they've previously experienced.

When the experience of trauma occurs, our fight or flight system is activated. With trauma or any experience that ignites a sense of fear or panic, our bodies either respond in preparation to fight, run, or freeze. If the situation leaves a psychological impact on us, our fight or flight functions can become desensitized or hypersensitive. We can constantly be on edge looking out for emotional or physical threats. We can perceive an interaction to be a threat when it's not because our minds are hypersensitive or "extra "cautious. We can also be emotionally detached from stimuli that would typically cause fear or panic because our fight or flight system has become too activated in the past, and the best way for us to protect ourselves is to emotionally shut down so that we don't deal with pain.

For someone who has grown up in, or has had multiple experiences in having exposure to or involvement in abuse, your brain functions a bit differently than someone who has not had the same experiences. The way you process safety is different. The means that you go about ensuring your sense of safety is different. Because a sense of fear underlines all your interactions, you may find yourself being overly agreeable, self-sacrificing, or forgiving, as to not upset others, in hopes that they don't cause you harm. You essentially play peacemaker and present as pleasantly as possible, as to ensure that no one will do anything to say or hurt you. You can also be on the other side of the coin, where you take control of relationships, and often engage as an aggressor, likewise to protect yourself, so that no one can say or do anything to harm you. Experiencing abuse can leave you feeling helpless; however, helplessness does ensure survival, so your brain uses its internal resources to ensure, what is the best way I can stay alive?

Even if its' been years beyond your experience of abuse, your body is hypervigilant and hypersensitive to the slight changes in others' body language or tone. You pick up cues in ways others don't, because you are now wired in a way that says the world and people around me are not safe. Beyond your hypervigilance, those emotions of fear may bring on anger, sadness, and shame, which consequently have long term impacts on your body. These emotions you have held on to if you have not processed the trauma can lead to chronic pains, cancers, cardiovascular diseases, immune illnesses and more. If you recall, when I discussed the ACE study in earlier, I shared how researchers found that having four or more adverse childhood experiences, increased one's chances of developing certain physical and mental health outcomes, it is because of this mind-body connection.

If the experience of certain emotions poses a threat to or compromises any of your internal systems to overwork, they may eventually weaken and increase the chances of certain physical ailments. In 2014, psychiatrist Bessel van der Kolk published the highly esteemed and groundbreaking book; The Body Keeps the Score[vii]. In it, Van der Kolk provides great detail on his research in working with individuals with Post Traumatic Stress Disorder.

He shares how his research reveals the complexities of the social, emotional, and mental health challenges, which come with surviving trauma. Due to the extent, there are long-lasting impacts on sleep, concentration, problem-solving, relationship building, goal setting, intimacy, and chronic pain. We know that trauma has many physical effects because research has shown that the body keeps score of what it has endured.

The source of the trauma can create different types of responses and physical experiences. Trauma-based in the body such as that caused by physical abuse, sexual abuse/assault, burning, gunshot, stabbing, or by some type of force is literally held within the body. These experiences leave behind both physical and emotional wounds.

With all this information, the question is, *how do you heal? How do you learn how to honor your body, despite the trauma it is has survived?*

We go back to the 4 A's. Let's look at acknowledgment and acceptance. Healing always begins with acknowledgement and acceptance. What is done has passed. The pain continues to live thru, and as hurtful as that reality is, it's possible to find a sense of accountability in you connecting to your current power. You have the will and tenacity to explore what it means to love and honor yourself, which means you are capable of gathering tools, of supporting you moving forward in your life.

Look at the residue that these experiences have left on your emotional body. *How does fear control you? How does the desire to control life, control you? What does relationship building look like? What do boundaries look like in order to preserve yourself?* You may have really porous boundaries or really rigid boundaries. You may not be able to be accurately processed when something or someone is safe and healthy due to the intense stimulation your system is used to having. You may "thrive" better in what looks like "dramatic" to someone else because the chemical response that your body needs to feel "alive" is manifested in being involved in emotionally and physically intense relationships or environments. We are not the results what happens to us. When tragedy strikes, its nothing we ask for, so it's not about holding ourselves accountable in a way that leads one to take responsibility for the actions of others; absolutely not. However, we can hold ourselves accountable for the power we utilize to propel our lives.

If you are aware that you have experienced trauma that has left an imprint on your emotional body, work to be gentle with yourself. Work on speaking gently to yourself. Work on processing the pain of the trauma and looking into activities that allow you to release it. Focus on self-care that allows you to shift what is going on in your Hidden Body.

Often times, somatic, body-based activities can help you move the impact of trauma. Movement, like dancing, walking or exercising (if appropriate), can be helpful. Finding a somatic therapist or experiencing body healing work thru massages, acupuncture, cupping, or chiropractor can be helpful. Exploring energy-based work like reiki or sound healing could be outlets. Sitting, walking or doing grounding exercises in nature, where your body can touch and interact with the ground, water, trees, or air is a possibility. Positive sensory stimulation thru warm or cold baths or showers or even music are examples of such possibility.

Other coping tools look like praying, meditating, reading personal development books, getting rest, involving yourself in causes bigger than you, doing what I love like going to shows, and dancing, listening to positive music, and, most importantly, surrounding myself with positive individual.

Know that until you take action to constantly release the emotions that the traumas caused, your body will continue to manifests ailments as a result of the trauma. Honoring your body is being sensitive to what you have lived thru, and be intentional about what you expose yourself to and even being mindful of who you allow in your personal space. People and experiences can easily be triggers and easily activate trauma responses, thus creating more tension, imbalance, and chaos within your body. Be mindful of being around people, places, and objects that nurture your body. Be mindful of staying away from people and environments that reflect your emotional wounds or trauma; they become an irritant. Select people and environments that feel safe and comforting.

Sometimes we may feel comfortable staying in contact with people or environments that resemble our wounds. It's as if our brains need that rush. It's as if we need to stay in the chaos, but that is not honoring your body. Learn to walk away and stay distant from stimuli that you know are triggering. It's important to note that, in reality, you will not be able to avoid being triggered. You will see and hear things that may activate your body to re-live a traumatic experience. With that exposure, it's important to honor your body still, remind yourself that you are safe, and practice necessary coping skills to regulate yourself.

Body image

How do you talk to your body? How do you see your body? How do you feel about your body? How do you speak life into your body? Honoring your body includes understanding that the perception of your body and the words that you speak to or against it, affects your body image. The conceptualization of body image and the relationship that one has with their body is complex. It provides a massive problem for women. Women are constantly comparing themselves to other women. There is constant exploration and fixation of ways to improve or alter the natural states of the body. Many want to take away, nip, tuck, or cover up what is naturally given. Many are ashamed to show their bodies. Many are ashamed to look at their bodies. Some elevate their bodies to the point that it is praised and adored; the body that they've been able to attain ushers them to shame others because they don't look like or dress like them. People begin to judge others.

Do you accept and embrace your body in its current state? How comfortable are you if you didn't enhance your body in any way? Do you look at your body in its glory and say I love you? Do you praise and admire the beauty of your body? If the answer is no, or you find it difficult to do any of those mentioned above, let's talk about the difficulty. *Why are you ashamed of your body in its natural state? Why are you critical of the scars, dimples, or excess skin that you have?* When it comes to standards of beauty, one must realize that they are ideals that a small fraction of people actually reflect. Consider that more people must take measures to manipulate their bodies (face and hair included) and intentionally work towards a goal (in food and fitness) to meet this ideal. When it comes to naturally meeting this ideal, it's almost not a reality without some type of force or manipulation. No one really fits the bill for the standards of beauty that many try to strive for.

It is a fact of the matter that all bodies do not look the same, nor are they meant to be alike. The physical experiences of our bodies are impacted by environment, food, movement, and heredity. A singular beauty ideal is not culturally competent. Values often shape how people experience life, and as the values of various cultures differ, so do the roles people play and the ideals around what they look like. Aspects of our physical appearance are praised across cultures. A comparison that leads to dissatisfaction is often based on exposure to ideal body types. As the US is often a leader in global media, there are many images portrayed for those who live in the US, as well as abroad, as to what is ideal and accepted. Everything from fashion to body type portrayed in print and visual media shapes the minds of others.

The US is a mixing bowl of many different cultures and ethnicities, which also gives way to all types of shapes and sizes. This tends to be a sensitive area for women, so that is what I will focus on. For many years, specific body types were promoted in media, often reflective of a slender frame. Others' bodies were not included or often ridiculed. Whether at the end of what is seen or not seen, exclusion and promotion of particular body types impact one's body image. Beyond body shape, there are judgments of skin complexion as well as hair type. There's impact in not seeing features that are similar or representative of who you are; it leads you to believe that what you present as is not acceptable. Just like fashion trends, the promotion of body types, or specific features go in and out of style; they are on and off trend. In the US, buying into an ideal body has been a movement that has impacted by advocates that promote a healthy, accepting, transformative perspective of body.

People spend hundreds and thousands of dollars to enhance their body to reflect trending body types. Consequently people are dying to look like a trending body type. What is the motivation for the enhancement? Is it for confidence? Is it driven by a desire to please others or gain appraisal by others? If you're enhancing your body due to an accident or an unfortunate circumstance, you may never truly be able to see yourself for who you are you are more than your body. If you have challenges praising, uplifting and loving your body, your mind is affected by that, your spirit is affected by that, your ability to let go is affected by that, your ability to forgive is affected by that, and clearly, the ability to just accept your full self is affected by that.

Sexual Health

Sex and self-love can be a very complicated topic to discuss. Sex is simple, but the attitude that one has toward sex makes it a complicated topic. Humans are driven by their ability and desire to survive and reproduce. From an evolutionary standpoint, sex serves two purposes: one is for human reproduction and the second serves as a function of intimacy so that the human specimen can feel safe. As humans, we have developed societies, organizational structures, and communities. Our understandings of ourselves, our bodies, and our functions have expanded over time. Sex is a simple part of life; however, depending on your cultural or religious perspectives, the narrative that one holds around sex can be impacted, be skewed, or complicated.

My attempt to speak about sex and self-love is in no way intended to deter or distract anyone from the rules that govern their own personal sex life. However, I will speak on the matter of self-love when it comes to sex. As sex is an extension of both how you can honor your body and spirit; hence, it's essential to our conversation.

Beyond the biological functions of sex, it's important to understand that sex in each individual's life takes on particular symbolism and meaning. It's always important to remember and understand as with most concepts and factors that impact life choices; there doesn't have to be one way or one lens to view sex thru. Like most concepts in life impacted by human behavior, looking at sex thru the lens of self-love is extremely multifaceted.

As a vessel, your body holds your spirit; likewise, it holds the functioning of your being. The brain has pleasure and reward systems, which are connected to the sexual experience. The endocrine system produces hormones upon arousal, aiding in the sexual experience. Our bodies are intelligent machines. However, it is our decisions, experiences, and mentality around sex that impacts our relationships with our body and its divine wisdom.

Despite the pleasure that can be experienced from sex, it is not a pleasurable experience for everyone. In many cultures, sex and the body comes with politics and norms of acceptance as well as deviance. When someone is lead to believe that they don't have agency over their body because of laws or dogma, sex is not seen as pleasurable; nor is the body is seen as a source of pleasure. It can be difficult to honor or connect to your body if it is seen as a tool, an object, or a symbol of shame. Learning how to honor the body can provide a personal revolution of sorts. It can be act of defiance if you're in a culture that sets forth the narrative that your body is not something for you to feel connected to or empowered by.

It's important always to consider *what has shaped my perspective of myself? What has shaped my perspective of life? In the case of the sex and the body, what has shaped my understanding of relationship with sex and my body?* Our understanding of and relationship with our bodies are primarily influenced by these sculptors and norms. As with the other commandments, the ability to honor ourselves even in the realm of sex is an act of self-love. This can be extremely difficult and

161

complicated, depending on the lens in which you view or have a connection to agency. If you do not have freedom or perceive that you have freedom to truly embrace, accept, and honor your body than this could prove to be a challenging commandment for you. Otherwise, you can ask yourself the following questions. *How do you revere, connect to or accept your body in its sexual form? How do you connect to your sense of self as a sexual being? How do you honor your sexuality?*

The body is something to be celebrated for its miraculous offerings. It allows us to live life as a means of sharing ourselves with the world. We have the ability to adorn it however we choose. We have the ability to use it in whatever way we choose. We have the ability to embrace it however we choose. In its functioning, it is also a temple of beauty and possible exploration. As one can mindfully engage in their environment or even with food, one can be with and in their body mindfully. Exploring your body and understanding how it operates sexually, is another means of connecting to yourself.

To understand anything, one must be curious, inquisitive, and explorative in nature. When learning about subject matters, you may do research, raise questions, and look for the answers. It is a similar process when learning about yourself. You ask questions.

You gather information about your life and what has shaped you, in order to be clearer on your own motivations and influences. When it comes to getting to know your body, you can collect information from books, but its best to pay attention to what your body does, what it longs for, what repels it, or what even puts it out of balance. Understanding your body includes sexual arousal and reaction.

A distorted sense of one's sexual nature occurs when one decides to look at themselves thru the eyes or perspective of another. When referencing "another" that could be someone of interest, media, and doctrine of sort, or even family, friends, or other social connections. Information about yourself is available to you when you spend time with yourself, or even being mindful of how your body responds around various stimuli.

It is far too often that individuals experience the body and sex from a place of coercion, manipulation, control, and/or judgment. It is common that in the US, a young person's first sexual experience is brought on by "random encounter" under misleading or ambivalent circumstances. Developmentally, it is normal for children between the ages of 5-8 to touch or raise questions about their various body parts in order to grow in understanding about their world, and all that is in it. It is developmentally inappropriate for children to be exposed to candid acts or images of sex, or the body being oversexualized for pleasure, e.g. pornography. Far too often, young children are approached by adolescents and adults and are taken advantage of. Far too often, young children are sexually misused, defined to include rape, molestation, and/or incest. In the US, it is estimated that 1 out 4 girls and 1 out of 6 boys are sexually misused. The result is often shame or hypersexualized perceptions of their body, others' bodies, and the role that pleasure plays.

As young impressionable beings, children can also be exposed to norms that criminalize and demonize sexual expression. This begins to shape the child's perception of sex as unnatural, "bad," dangerous or forbidden. For some, this leads to a complete connection to the sexual nature that naturally exists. Some may see it difficult in finding or experiencing pleasure. For others, the taboo of sex makes it all the more desirable. A lifestyle of deprivation can lead someone into developing intense urges, and lack self-control or moderation, once they are exposed to the very stimulus which has been off limits. For some, sex is never enough; there is always more to get. In any mental state that is driven by excess and lack of control, the person engaging in the act, has a difficult time actually connecting with whatever the source of their motivation is.

Using any coping tool that masks what an emotional experience is, as opposed to learning to process and regulate ones' self is problematic. Sex is often a coping tool used to mask emotion. People go to sex when feeling lonely, abandoned, unloved, angry, unworthy, sad, and afraid. This is not how you honor yourself or your body. All emotions experienced can be held within the body or even transferred on to other beings, as they are all bound by energy. When you use your body as a vessel to transfer energy, you get to choose which level of frequency you are transferring. You using someone for pleasure or to release your emotions of fear, loneliness, etc. not only doesn't truly heal in you in the end but actually can impact the other person or persons.

The ability to provide sexual pleasure to others is something that defines many peoples worth and value as an individual and in relationships. People use sex to manipulate others to do what they want. They practice of controlling another by giving or withdrawing sex from a partner as a means of positive or negative reinforcement of behaviors. One can find a sense of value in their ability to control or influence another's behaviors because of their sexual abilities. On the opposite, one may determine another's value or worth based on their ability to please, or at least on how the appearance or presence of their body can stimulate the desire to receive sexual pleasure.

Sex can be a path of intimacy, but it is not the only or ultimate path to build intimacy with another; therefore, someone people use sex as the basis of the relationships when they do not know how or are too afraid of building intimacy thru vulnerability and communication. When couples experience emotional and communication challenges, both or one may use sex as a means of control, encouragement or punishment for another. Using your sexual skills does not solve emotional issues. It does not heal someone who feels ignored, unheard or disrespected, and it will not heal you. Using sex is not the sure way to open someone up to express to you how they really feel. Sex does not replace partners being open and honest about their feelings around a subject or with one another. Despite the notion that physical touch is a major love language, and can be a primary way that someone can express their affection, it does not replace how you treat someone, or how someone treats you. Sex can impact connection, but it is not the sole foundation on which connection can be based.

What about shame or guilt that comes along with different aspects of the body and sex? How can the experiences of shame, guilt, or anger impact sex and how one honors the body? If you experience anything that brings on shame, meaning self-inflicted character assassination in relation to a decision made, you may hide from, minimize engagement in, or deny self of sex. Shame can come from surviving sexual assault, impotence, disfiguring, sexual performance, knowledge or skills, or acquiring an STD/STI. Guilt can ensue if you harm or dishonor another in any kind of way in relation to sex or the body. One can feel shame or guilt even having sex while pregnant, or in the thought or attempt of having sex after giving birth. The experience of having sex with people or a certain person for any number of reasons can bring along shame/guilt. Sex, after the dissolution of a relationship or losing a partner physically, can ring about guilt or shame. Anger can be experienced as a result of an outside circumstance motivating to use sex to either relieve yourself or cause harm or send a message to another.

It becomes dishonoring to yourself when you minimize your value-based on your sexual capacity. It becomes dishonoring to your body when you minimize its value based on the pleasure it provides yourself or another. The body and its purpose are multifaceted. The essence of you cannot be contained or defined by the chemicals your body produces, the muscle contractions that occur, or the feelings of your reproductive organs during moments of pleasure. Your value goes beyond the dimensions of the body parts on you that are seen as symbols of pleasure. Due to the complexity of the relationships we have with our bodies, it's so important to remember that it is just one aspect of your being.

Mindfully Moving the Body

Honoring your body thru the power of movement can help harness a beautiful relationship between you and your body. Movement does not have to be qualified as intense or exercise. Its taking parts of our bodies from a place of stillness, and harnessing the power that our limbs, muscles, ligaments, and joints, come together to allow us to have. There is so much power that stillness can offer as we work on mindfulness practices, however, if we have the capacity to move our bodies, it would always serve us to take advantage of that gift.

We often unconsciously move our bodies when completing tasks that we often take for granted, like brushing teeth, smiling, eating or opening a door. For most individuals, these movements are not thought about. We engage in this movement with little insight, reflection, gratitude or mindfulness. *Would you know how to open a door or eat mindfully?* Mindful movement is all about engaging with your senses and being aware of what is going on. If one day you were able to walk with no assistance, pain, discomfort, or overall difficulty, then got in a car accident and had to wear a cast, I assure you, your relationship to movement and your body would be different.

Individuals that have injuries and disabilities that impact their movement and mobility tend to be more mindful of their movement because some of their day to day experience is obstructed by their physical limitations. Someone healing from an injury may look forward to the day that their injured body part can function healthily again. Someone with a physical disability may constantly be reminded of their challenges if they are constantly around able-bodied people. There is a different consideration or focus on the complexity and agility of the body when one considers they may have limitations. Beyond an injury or disability, mindfulness of the body may also shift as one age. In youth, mobility comes easy; however, as you get older, you notice your joints are more sensitive or may get stiff easier.

Being able to move mindfully means to be grounded in the present with your body and the gifts that it brings.

Mobility may be one of the many gifts that you take granted. However, in self-love, we don't minimize anything. We acknowledge, celebrate, and cheer ourselves and others on. Honor your body with movement, to keep your blood flowing. Honor your body with movement, to show gratitude for the agility that you do have.

When it comes to movement, many people tend to focus on exercise. Exercise, of course, has its benefits; however, many people do not focus on pure benefits. They focus on exercise as a means to obtain what they may want: acceptance from others, or satisfaction with self by obtaining a specific body type. This is, of course, a book about self-love, so I wouldn't say don't work out if it makes you feel good, but questioning the intention, and assessing your attachment to what working out represents to you matters.

According to Market Data LLC, a research company that comprises annual research on various industries reports that the weight loss industry is now worth a record $72 billion[viii]. Even though "diet" trends are down, one of the many contributing factors is the rise in use of fitness trackers. Individuals continue to become increasingly fixated on fitness. Fitness for a means of normal recommended activity, versus vanity driven acceptance are different types of fitness. There are so many positive benefits to fitness. Fitness is beneficial for your physical, as well as your mental health.

"We've known for some time that exercise has a role to play in treating symptoms of depression, but this is the first time we have been able to quantify the preventative potential of physical activity in terms of reducing future levels of depression," said by lead author Associate Professor Samuel Harvey from Black Dog Institute and UNSW. "These findings are exciting because they show that even relatively small amounts of exercise -- from one hour per week -- can deliver significant protection against depression[ix]." Fitness, otherwise known as an intentional movement for the body, is important. Everyone's ability to move or navigate their body is different. If you are an able-bodied individual to any capacity, being able to connect with your body as it moves is such an amazing experience.

Fitness can be a great motivator to help individuals work on skills and qualities like focus, goal setting, resilience, and determination. Fitness can give individuals a sense of accomplishment. However, intention and moderation matter. You can move thru walking, running, dancing, cycling, swimming, skipping, jumping, and so much more. Fitness is a great way for us to push ourselves to places that we didn't consider reaching at previous times in life. Fitness allows us to gauge where we are, set goals and move toward something greater in the future. However, fitness can become a dangerous obsession when we feel that our worth and our value is tied up in our ability to reach a fitness or body goal.

There is the possibility of having an unhealthy relationship with exercise. When one is overly fixated on exercising, excessively exercising throughout the day and week, and compromises the quality of a well-rounded life for the sake of exercising, that is when it is time to re-assess. As a mental health clinician that has supported individuals with eating disorders, I can assure you that sometimes, one's relationship with exercising can begin healthily and truly evolve into an unhealthy obsession. Within the last 15 years, mental health therapists and medical doctors have come to understand the growing presence of what has been labeled as Orthorexia. Orthorexia is proposed eating disorder characterized by an excessive preoccupation with eating healthy food and often accompanied by excessive exercising. It is not recognized as an official disorder in the Diagnostic Statistical manual; however, many health care providers working with clients with disordered eating or even body dysmorphia, are able to recognize when a client falls into this category.

Too much of anything that leads to depletion, restriction, self-hatred, increase in isolation, or social anxiety cannot be considered healthy. To honor your body with mindful movement is to be connected to the gifts that can come from your body's strength. It's your opportunity to connect to the miracles that your body can produce. Movement is not about judgment. If movement included judgement, it would not be honoring yourself or your body. Movement is not just about exercise. Consider if you're looking at someone else's pictures or body, and you imagine how hard you need to work to look like them. When we create this narrative, that movement mainly serves an ego, re-grounding and being mindful of who we really are; is essential. One can get to the point in which they believe their worth is tied to the quantity, duration, difficulty or frequency of exercising. One can develop an internal system of judgment towards others who don't exercise as much or have the same dedication towards it.

Exercise is about taking care of our temple. Our bodies are temples housing our spiritual selves, spiritual beings having an earthly experience. We need our bodies to carry us thru this life. As we see our bodies as homes, we can take steps to care for our homes. Just remember, movement is more than exercising to look a certain way or fit a particular outfit. You move to dance, to hold your loved ones, to cook, to clean, to be productive in work, and to keep your blood flowing. I want to make it very clear that I intend to emphasize movement and not just emphasize exercise. In relation to exercise, I do not speak of fitness to support any aesthetic goals or ideas that one might have. If you use exercise as a means to obtain a certain aesthetic, that is your decision, however, be mindful of how you honor yourself and even practice forgiveness. Be mindful, how you speak to yourself when you don't meet a fitness goal, or your body doesn't look like how you want it. Be mindful of the level of aggression or gentleness you show yourself. Be mindful if you fall into spaces of comparison.

If you find yourself falling in a harsh, critical, or judgmental space, take a step back, and think of the gratitude you have for the functions of your body. Think about the activities that you are grateful that your body allows you to do. Consider all the life that your body has endured. Learn to hug your body. Learn to engage your senses as you do simple tasks. Connect to your senses as you walk, speak, eat, or simply type. Be mindful of low impact, intentional movements. Engage in movement to connect with your body; honor it as it is, as opposed to constantly focusing on why it isn't good enough.

Nourishing the Body

Speaking from the lens of someone raised in the US, I can say that most people in the US have an unhealthy relationship with food. Most people don't understand how the body, let alone how nutrition works. Beyond science, exploring our relationship is vital. Our relationship with food begins as a child. We learn our eating habits from our parents and pick up cues from how they use food to reinforce behaviors, or even encourage restriction. Think of the many tactics that parents may use with children.

When you are sad, you may get a treat to make you feel better. When you do something well, you get a treat to celebrate. Some parents require eating at the table for a more formal experience with family. Others may let children eat in front of the TV, or alone in their room. If you have a "negative" behavior, you don't get to eat the food you like. If you have a dislike for a certain food, a parent may force you to eat it. A parent may over monitor your food, and dissuade you from getting seconds. A parent may not allow a child to connect to their fullness cues by encouraging them to "eat all their food" despite a child saying they're full.

Aside from how a parent monitored a child's eating, there are behaviors that a child witnesses. Some parents are frequent dieters; they are always talking about a different diet, or the child witnesses them commenting on the effectiveness of their different diets. Parents who may exclude food groups. Parents who restrict the consumption of certain types of food. Parents who make comments that certain food may directly link to specific changes in the body. Parents who are very vocal about "good and bad" foods. Parents who engage in rarely eating or eating small amounts of food. Parents who engage in overeating, or grazing throughout the day.

Children are rarely taught how to be intuitive eaters and to follow their hunger and fullness. Children aren't often taught how to be mindful eaters and engage with their food thru their senses. Busy parents have to rush children to hurry up and eat breakfast, eat it on the go, or not eat it at all because they don't have time. Children may develop the habit of only eating snacks during the day at school, and not eating a balanced meal until dinner.

These types of practices lead to many narratives about foods. We learn to lean on food for comfort. When things are bad, go-to food. When things are good, go-to food. For some, they develop a relationship that sees food as punishment. If they do something "bad," there are certain foods they don't get to have. Having certain foods is bad, and if they have those foods, they are bad. We learn to eat in solitude and mindlessly. We learn that food is a requirement, but not something to be enjoyed. Food is only for nourishment, or a tool to obtain an ideal body. We learn that supplements and liquid food are more important than getting nutrients from whole foods. We learn that we cannot trust ourselves with food. We learn that if there is food in front of you, you must eat it, regardless of how you feel about it.

Food may be accompanied by judgment. Caregivers, family members, or peers may have made statements about how you eat when you eat, and how much you eat. Coupled with complements or judgments, possibly about your body, your mind creates an unhealthy connection between both your eating and your body. Food can also be accompanied by unpleasant memories. Certain meal times may represent conflict and pain in the home. If you grew up under the circumstances with limited resources, food may not seem like a necessity or can be perceived as something associated with excess. As we grow, our life experiences may continue to perpetuate these narratives that began at a younger age. We are inundated with images and content that promotes diet culture or a focus on what and how much we eat. We may continue to foster unhealthy habits and relationships with foods, with no one around us to point them out and make us accountable.

These are the many pathways that I've witnessed individuals with disordered eating travel down as their illnesses strengthened. One may develop unhealthy relationships with food during the adolescence, and with the average person not really paying attention to how others eat, the problem continued to worsen. *How does one learn to mend their relationship with food?*

There are many questions you can ask yourself when it comes to your relationships with food.

What role does food play in my life?

How would I describe my relationship with food?

When do I know I am hungry or full?

What food rules do I have? Where did they come from?

What foods do I gravitate toward? Why?

What foods do I keep distant from? Why?

Are there foods I see as special, Bad, Good, Healthy, or Unhealthy?

As I previously mentioned with movement and fitness, look at your intention. Look at your why. When you tend to lean towards a certain action around food, whether it's eating, not eating, eating more, eating less. Whether you're labeling something good or bad, ask why. The intention always matters, and to heal or shift anything, the truth must always be acknowledged first.

Let food be thy medicine; do not let medicine be thy food. We are in a time where cardiovascular diseases are at an all-time high; diabetes, cancer, obesity are plaguing people at an extremely alarming rate. This isn't because our bodies are evolving, and they are malfunctioning. No. These conditions and illnesses are often brought on by lifestyles. We have lifestyle changes that compared to hundreds of years ago, and have put our bodies at risk for failure; our organ systems and our cell functioning are at risk of failure.

Nutrition – We hear the term, but we don't consider what it really means. Often people eat mindlessly, drink their beverages mindlessly, and consume supplements mindlessly. Food is treated like a reward system. "I had this type of week, so I deserve this." "This is going on in my life, so I deserve this." However, when we eat, we are mindful of the reward center in our mind being pleasured, but we do not always take into account how our food is affecting our body.

Now, of course, everyone is raised in different households with various eating styles. Unlike many countries and cultures, we don't particularly have a standard American diet in the US. We have vegan, vegetarian, paleo, pescatarian, omnivore, low fat, high protein, and "eat whatever I want" diets. There are households in which caregivers cook most days of the week, others in which fast food is the primary source of food and others where frozen food is the primary source of food. There are so many different lifestyles and choosing to honor your body thru nutrition is not necessarily about choosing just one lifestyle. I don't believe in promoting any particular lifestyle; however, I do believe in educating yourself on what's best for your body. I believe in you paying attention to your body's signals of energy, fatigue, sensitivity, digestion or inflammation.

If you walk into any American bookstore or even go to an online merchant that sells books on the topic of nutrition, you will come across hundreds of thousands of books, providing a recommendation on what and how to eat. Endless books are exploring various "diets" and all the foods to omit to obtain the "right" body. Discussing such matters can be dangerous because you never know how someone will really apply and use that information.

What is your relationship with the word diet?

The interesting thing about diet is that people use it as a verb when it is a noun. Everyone has a particular diet; however, the health and fitness industry has been so great at marketing the word diet to be specific to particular set of guidelines describing how someone eats. Our relationship with food has become so rigid when it would serve us to consider how and what we eat from different perspectives. Eating to enjoy and savor our food is important, as well as understanding the nutrients our bodies need in moderation. I believe that food can be your medicine. When we have access to nutrient-rich food and clean water, our bodies thrive off of that. It's important to pay attention to your bodies responses to food. Giving it to little or too much of anything may cause harm in ways that may not be visible or completely noticeable.

Your body is an advanced machine and knows what it needs. Developing a relationship with your body and honoring it, is about being able to pay attention to the small shifts without becoming fixated on everything. Your body has different ways of revealing what it needs. Whatever you intake, both solids and liquids affect your concentration, alertness, mood, and strength. Symptoms like constipation, nausea, gas, indigestion, loose bowels, acid reflux, and constant fatigue, are modes of communication from your body. Additional changes to

181

be mindful of are the color of your skin and eyes, complexion, strength of your hair and nails, the dryness or moisture of your skin, urine color, and composition of your bowels. Because everything is connected, any nutrients you require or experiencing an overproduction of will often reveal itself in your body processes.

You must come to understand what nourishes your body to allow you to thrive and be able to operate at your highest capacity. It may take time because if you have not had a strong relationship with your body, it is something you must work on. What works for someone else may not work for you because you two have completely different body chemistry. You have different needs based on factors like size, age, activity level throughout the day, personal medical history, climate/environment, and genetics.

Interacting with our food and beverages can provide an explorative experience if we allow it. As the practice of mindfulness can be integrated into many activities throughout our days, it can also be applied to how we interact. As a mental health clinician who has supported many individuals with eating disorders, I can say that the practice of mindful eating is a tool that can help re-acclimate, re-new, and even create a new relationship between a person and their food. Mindful eating is the process in which we allow ourselves to connect to our food and beverages. In mindfully eating, we consider the qualities of the food based on the stimulation of our senses. *How would you describe the texture, taste, color, and aroma of your food?* We also connect to the emotional experience we may have with food. *How does our food make us feel in the moment when we have it in our hands? How do we feel after consuming our food? How do we feel as our food is going thru the process of digestion?*

Yes, asking questions before, during, and after you eat is a part of the process of learning how to honor your body. Because we learn how to ignore and repress our emotions, we have no idea how much they truly impact our lived experience, and that includes with food. *Do you know how your emotions impact your experience with food?* As mentioned earlier, we often develop narratives around food and its functions based on the relationships our caregivers modeled and socialized us to believe in. How do you honor your body when you are sad? How do you honor your body when you are excited and want to celebrate? For many people, either of those emotional experiences would lead to food. However, when we use food to accompany and emotional experience, we must understand that food is literally being used as a tool or form of expression. You are consuming food, but it's more than food. The food is representing something for you.

Thru the programming you receive via the media, which assigns specific foods, liquids, or substances to be aligned with specific emotional experiences, you often develop habits, unknowingly. Beyond the basics of nutrition, many foods develop symbolism, and we create associations. Think I'm kidding? What does pumpkin or sweet potato pie bring up for you? What do you associate turkey with? What do you associate cake with? What comes up for you with the items fried oreo, cotton candy or funnel cake? What comes up for you when you see a pint of ice cream? What comes up when you see steak and lobster? What comes up for you when you think salad?

I would bet money that there was either a person, place, occasion, or holiday that came up at least once as you answered these questions. Maybe as the associations came to mind, you could feel your body warming up, getting goosebumps, or feeling tingly. It's possible that you began to salivate and think about possibly having any of these foods. It's possible that you went down memory lane. It's possible that you had positive or negative memories of these. The mere activations of thoughts and emotions at the sight of foods written out, speaks to how powerful of an impact that food has on us. This also speaks to how strongly connected the different aspects of our being and biology is. The sight of a word ignites emotions, thoughts, and physiological responses. If the sight of a word can do that, imagine what the aroma, sight, or taste of certain foods can do.

Some people's relationship with food is purely based on association, and they don't take in any real-time information that the experience with the food can provide. When we don't eat mindfully, we can automatically assume "we like something" just because we're comfortable with it; however, let time pass, and try to re-engage, sometimes it does not taste like how you "remember." After eating something that you haven't had in some time, you assume you would like it because of the emotional or mental association you had with the item but was not present to the fact that your taste buds change, and maybe your preferences or sensitivities for specific tastes have changed. This is the same type of association we can get with certain "comfort foods." We may have emotional attachment to certain foods because they used to provide so much comfort to us at particular stages in our lives, but if we are honest with ourselves, they may not be void of comfort, but they may even cause physical discomfort.

When it comes to much of the decisions we make, the intention is always something we can re-visit. When you eat food after rejection or someone physically leaves you, are you eating because you want the food? Or is it because you are hoping it makes you feel better due to feeling sad and alone? Even if the consumption of certain food brings positive emotion and gives you joy, but you notice that once you begin to digest it, you feel sluggish, ***do you know how to honor your body and stop interacting with the food, or do you keep going?*** Some individuals continue to eat past fullness or pass the point of comfort, and then experience guilty because they did so. One enters that cycle of self-degradation that was discussed previously.

If you know that ignoring your body's cues is going to lead you down a dark road, it's important to have the insight that supports you in stopping when necessary. For many, the dark road leads to a fixation on calories, worry, and concern about physical change that may take place as a result of the meal, or one may experience a complete shift in body image. Consider if these are thoughts or patterns you lean in to, after eating.

So much of how we relate to ourselves is routed thru our perception of and connection to our bodies. When it comes to how you engage in nutrition, whatever you choose as a path of honor in reflection of what you believe you deserve, ask if it is honoring to the experience of your elevation. If you can answer yes to the question, proceed. If you pause at any moment, or if your spirit seems uneasy, allow yourself to stop and reflect. Maybe the stop will be temporary, so you can become aligned with yourself, and flow in knowing that you can trust yourself and keep going. Or maybe the stop is final, and just like you would do with any other behavior or activity you found yourself sitting in dishonor, you can step away from the action, step away from the environment, step away from what you're doing and let it go.

Every item that you choose to eat or consume in any way has energy. We are consuming nutrients and energy, whether its food, herbs, medicine, dietary supplements or beverages. When we choose items that nourish us in the right way, we can choose nutrients that promote strength and vitality. Our nutrients have the power to combat and eliminate illnesses, but of course our intake is just one aspect of how we manage our health. It's really important to understand that this doesn't mean that it's bad to have fatty food nor to eat sugar. I surely believe that all food fits. We demonize certain foods when in reality, everything provides some type of nutrients. It's all about moderation.

Commandment 4: Honor Thy Spirit

Finding the Meaning of Spirit

Love and passion. Love and purpose. Love and intrigue. Love and family. Love and friends. Love and confusion. Love and security. Love and light. Love and darkness. Love and marriage. Love and infinity. Love and possibilities. Love and others. Love and self.

Self-love – Self in the role of love and love in the role of embracing and living thru self is essential for our elevation and being. The depth of our love can be strengthened by how we choose to honor our spirit.

The spirit can serve as a facilitator of love when it is fed in a way that supports both the gift and the receiving of love. From childhood, our spirit develops its sense of strength and identity. Whatever you feed lives properly and thrives. Whatever you starve and deprive, dies. Some spirits have been so distraught throughout the course of life that love seems like a foreign concept to their existence. These are the spirits that were not only surrounded by other dark spirits, but these are spirits that were beaten down by abuse, belittlement, and loneliness. Very little reinforcement of love, peace, and strength occurred throughout these experiences.

The spirit is a living entity harboring energy; therefore, its experience over the life span is one defined by a constant exchange of energy. Energy never stops. Consider the flow of going in and out. Energy follows a life`s formula of addition, subtraction, and multiplication. At this very moment, all the moments that have preceded it and all that comes after, your state of being and spirit is reflective of the energy which you have selectively and unknowingly absorbed. Every being you've interacted with, every conversation you've had, everything you've touched, smelled, listened to, tasted, and seen affect your energy and spirit.

Getting to the point where you move intending to honor your spirit is a very much developed skill. The more time you spend in meditation, the clearer you become. The more you can hear from the voice within, as opposed to the voices outside of you, the stronger your connection to self is. Remain in the knowing of what your spirit is telling you. Some people move in a way that allows them to interact with life as a game. They may take advantage of all people and opportunities that cross their paths. As a spirit-led and driven purpose, it is your task to learn how to discern when your spirit's voice is speaking loud enough to push you to move. Every experience or opportunity that presents itself is not aligned with you. Every presentation isn't for you; therefore, it does not serve or honor you to betray your spirit by being overly eager.

Being "hungry" for success is a common colloquialism nowadays. It can lead to a greedy, unfocused, and unintentional way of operating, depending on one's idea of success. When success is limitedly measured in terms of acquiring notoriety, wealth and assets, the hunger becomes dangerous. When the hunger may include impact of lives positively affected, or a positive legacy created, the hunger can be productive. It is the way of life of someone who's focus on material possessions and acquisitions, not the path of someone on personal and spiritual journey for elevation

Spirituality vs. Religion

As we have discussed, the spiritual dimension of yourself is one that is reflective of your metaphysical experience. It is beyond what your senses know to be true; however, your spiritual experience is impacted by what occurs thru your senses. In speaking of honoring thy spirit, or of the spirit in general, this is not necessarily related to the presence or practice of religiosity. Religion is a way of life that is chosen by a being. It is a set of principles, practices, and perspectives that guides their lives, and is heavily influenced by the rules and interpretation provided by other humans. It is more of an external process of understanding life. One's devotion to religiosity is based on a commitment to rituals and public displays of practice.

Spirituality is absolutely intuitive. It is an intuitive internal experience. It is a grounded connection to your intuitively higher self. It is a metaphysical explanation of your presence in the current realm. When we speak to spirituality, it's about your connection to yourself and is driven by who you are not, not who someone or an institution is telling you to be. In speaking of religiosity, we're speaking of an organized way of living. Spirituality is something we are born with, which is not dictated by someone else. Spirituality is an internal metaphysical experience that we have without the direction of dogma or principles.

Honor thy spirit is a commandment of importance because when we are learning to own our truths when we are learning to walk in our truths, and unapologetically be ourselves, we must really know and connect to who ourselves are. Being able to understand spirituality and what it means to honor your spirit is the gateway into you understanding how to love yourself; to acknowledge what you need and what your spirits needs. When we speak to spirituality, it's about your connection to your higher self.

It is the ability for you to be able to connect to your higher self and answer the question, "why," answer the question, "does this serve me?" We know the answers to our questions if we're able to sit still, be centered, and listen to our spiritual beings. It is the chaos and pandemonium created by external influences, options, and obligations that create our confusion.

We must remember that we know the answers, which is why religions across ways of life, across time, have always spoken to an internal and higher state of knowing and consciousness. This state of knowing is harnessed in a meditative, prayer, or hypnosis state. Whether we draw truth and clarity from nature, a deity, or some symbolic figure, the truth is once we get past the internal and external chatter, we find the answers to the questions we ask.

Zora Neale Hurston wisely said, "There are years that ask questions and years that answer." The same can be said for seasons and various moments in our life. No matter if we feel like the answers are far from us, it always just takes time to pay attention to how life leads us to what we are looking for. The great Rumi said, "What you are seeking is seeking you."

Grounded in Spirit

In February 2016, I had a beautiful experience with nature. I spent five days at a resort and bio conservative university in the rain forests of Costa Rica. My intention for the trip was to explore, relax, and possibly take in something beautiful that would breed transformation. Even though I knew I was in a rain forests region, I hoped for dry days filled with lots of sunshine; instead I got what I wanted, mixed with a lot of rain. Fortunately for me, it wasn't just any kind of rain. It wasn't the type of rainfall I'm used to in Los Angeles, where it sporadically drizzles (and we call it rain) at one point of the day, and then I'm met with sunshine. This was a rain forest region. It rains to nourish the land, and it surely poured throughout the whole day. Now if I were home, I would definitely remain indoors, just looking outside my window, thinking of all the things I could have done or wanted to do if it wasn't raining.

However, I embraced it. I embraced the rain to experience the wanderlust that I set out to experience in Costa Rica. Not only did I embrace the rain, but I felt that it offered me just what I needed. Amidst the rain, my trip went on. Every day, myself and the group I traveled with continued to engage in our scheduled itinerary and use what we could so the rain wouldn't impede our experience as much. We had hats, ponchos, and umbrellas. We toured our property in the rain. We zip lined in the rain. We walked from our rooms to our dining area in the rain for several mornings. Dare I say; it was beautiful!

I recall the first morning I began my day with yoga. It was under a covering of wood and long grass on top of a wood deck sitting beside a river. Aside from the beach back home, I had never done yoga in a natural setting. I was used to being at home or in a studio doing poses with zen music or nature sounds playing in the background. Typically, a nature soundscape audio track had the sounds of rainfall, wind, chimes, and various animal sounds in the background. However, this experience was different because I was amid nature's symphony. I had the honor of being outside with the rain, birds, crickets, and everything else that emitted sound during my experience.

It felt heavenly and magical. I felt a sense of groundedness that I had not experienced in previous yoga sessions. I felt warm, nostalgic, joyful, and completely grateful. It transformed my yoga experience. I was able to see the beauty of the rain and how connected everything was.

This one experience set the tone for my whole trip. Learning how to be present and pay attention to the lessons that nature is offering. It was such a key experience in my journey of self-love, transformation, and healing. I became more aware of how to re-ground myself to the Earth and pay attention to the miracles around. I became more aware of looking outside myself when I want to complain and pay attention to what's happening around me. This was an experience that absolutely nurtured my spirit. For me, it also solidified why exploring and being in outside is so important for my emotional and spiritual health.

Throughout these moments, I re-realized how blessed I was. Any moment, experience, or interaction of our life can introduce and re-confirm life lessons that lead us to a higher experience. I witnessed the beauty of life, transformation, breath, freedom, and nature. I often recall to myself how beautiful a teacher nature can be, and she always reminds me. On this trip, she reminded me of how simple and essential it is to be grounded in the spirit. To be so close to the Earth, in daily interaction, in constant appreciation of its miraculous processes brought to conscious the many reasons in how I can honor my spirit and myself.

There is always a duality that exists in life and in our existence. Give and receive; light and darkness; sow and reap; live and die; rain and sunshine. Accepting that life goes on and continues to progress no matter how involved or removed from what's going on is not only humbling but also reassuring that everything works out, serves a purpose, and has such a grander meaning beyond my or your conceptualization. I, like many others, tend to contemplate, plan, contemplate some more, and execute as efficiently as possible. Even though in most ways this process helps me fulfill what I believe to be a purpose-driven life, I know that my effort matters every step of the way and not just in execution. When plants grow, humans usually just take the stage of growth that the plant is in, for face value. We rarely consider the process. We don't consider the climate that supports the transformation of a seed or pedal to blossom into a fruit, flower, tree or bus. We don't consider the amount of rain or sunshine needed to help the specimen thrive. Many times, we don't even know that nature's farmers like ants, bees or hummingbirds are so connected to the process that without them, our world would be different.

To take this and allow myself to be grounded in spirit means to stay in the space of awareness remembering that life is a process. I matter in all capacities, and everything around me is connected for a purpose. At any point when I do not feel centered, it's easy to get caught up in a stream of thoughts and questions like: what's "happening TO me," "What can I control," "What do I have to stay" busy doing for my life to thrive? To be grounded in spirit, is to embrace the complexity of life and the connection of every moment.

To know the spirit is to connect to a sense of existence beyond your five senses. Even though spirit is impacted by the stimuli we receive with our senses, spirit detects the intangible and non-observant. Spirit connects to energy because, in its essence, spirit is energy. We are energy in a body that has been designed to be a complicated, self-running machine.

Connections to a rather indefinite and intangible force within ourselves allows a powerful yet not overbearing force within us to express itself, flow, and take its place in the circle of life. Humans study everything to obtain answers. Because of our cognitive capabilities, we want answers to everything. We crave information to describe a disconnected past, to deal with the present, and control the future. But nature teaches us just to be. Accept our purpose, grow and die.

How does one ground themselves? How do you ensure the peace of your spirit? Intentionality and openness are essential. Our thoughts and emotions are also energy. Therefore the stronger the energy fields around our thoughts and emotions, the stronger the magnetism to make those assumptions, fears, and desires real. When we pay attention to what is manifesting in our lives, we will find it is often a reflection of the fear, worry, joy, love, or desire we have. One of the highest frequencies experienced energetically is that of gratitude. Gratitude is such a beautiful practice and engages both your brain and your spirit.

Those special moments I had in Costa Rica were all about gratitude. I was grateful to be where I was, deepen my relationship with nature, and experience the connection between human experience and a non-human experience. Notions of the spirit are about cultivating connections beyond sensory knowledge. In these experiences, while in Costa Rica, I felt at one with so much beyond me as well as with myself, simultaneously. It was surely a bubble that somewhat got popped when I returned to the hustle and bustle of the city. However, I moved forward knowing the gifts and lessons that nature offers.

It became clear that being in nature, being surrounded by natural landscapes, is a tool of transformation, coping, grounding, and spirituality that many who live in majorly industrialized areas often forget. Those who are connected to the land, who stay connected to metaphysical walks of spirituality or energy sources understand the impact that being in nature offers. Being in the environment, I was in allowed me to connect to the land in a way that my higher consciousness had not done in many years. Walking away from that trip, not only did I come to understand how important travel for me was, but how much of a transcendent experience I personally realize when nature is my primary environment.

Every time I go on adventures, big or small, in exploration of answers and insight, not only do I receive the pearls of wisdom I have sought, but I always feel closer to God. I do believe in the power that awe offers. Being a small specimen in compared to 100-foot trees, large snow-covered mountain ranges, millennia-old canyons, or vast bodies of waters, always leave me spellbound as to the beauty, complexities and unexplainable connects that exists in this universe.

It's important to note that spirituality is not about cognition. It's not about what makes sense rationally. There is infinite intelligence available to us, and it isn't all about what we know and can tangibly describe. This is why I believe, someone not understanding the essence of who they are, can offer grand complexities in navigating life. People spend so much time focusing on who they are not, in comparison to who or what others are, all along, being disconnected from their power, infinite power, and knowledge. Many are driven and motivated by the norms they have been accustomed to, or by the wounds that drive them to strive for validation and importance in the eyes of others.

Honoring thy spirit is important to self-love because you can be connected to your spirit; you can also learn how to be connected with yourself. You can learn to trust yourself and not be swayed by the pressures of others. You can learn to connect to inner and higher wisdom, as you make steps towards walking the unique path that is meant for you. To cultivate a sense of connection to yourself, I would offer that is important to create moments where you can do so. Create moments of stillness and quiet time. Be alone with your own emotions and thoughts, so you can learn how to filter between what is yours, and what is in you as a consequence of your lived experience in this world.

Connecting to the Divine in You

God dwells in me, as me. When I speak of God, it is in reference to a divine force not bound by dogma or human understanding. Not bound by human construction of a masculine or feminine being. That is my perspective. There is some great and powerful force that exists within you, me, and all of us. There is something that connects all life together. Imagine the complexity of what it takes for your body to operate seamlessly and without intention or thought the way that it does. There is a force within you.

What allows you to think about a thing or person and it arrives or shows up within a respected time to get you to say, Oh that's funny, I was just thinking x,y,z. That is a great and powerful force. What allows a mother to nurture, incubate, and deliver life from her? That is a force.

Whatever someone's religious or spiritual affiliation lies is not my concern. However, knowing that some great and powerful force exists within you is important to me. This force, which I will call the divine, far surpasses the human experience. It is the force that awakens your 6th sense and permits you to consider that there is life beyond us and that the spirit realm is not imaginary. It allows you to connect your basic sensory experience and be at one with inexplainable. It is the force that guides your internal system, which permits you to say, "Positives vibes" or that someone's energy is "bad or good." These are not just words that we say. These are terms used to explain phenomena that we didn't necessarily feel comfortable with sharing at one time. Being able to listen to that intuitive yet non-audible voice in you is one way to connect to the divine in you.

Understanding that there are manifestation powers within you is another mode of connecting to the divine in you. As mentioned before, in our most simple state, we are a collection of energy. We are waves of frequency communicating with other waves of frequency. Imagine in the absence of words, with our pure thoughts or emotions; we can send signals out to the world and bring to pass some of our deepest desires. We can also in a very unexplainable way send what Hollywood would call "telepathic" messages to one another. How would you describe the rare times of someone close to you, "reading your mind" and calling just when you thought of them? When focused or intentional, we have telekinetic connections with others.

Understanding that there is a harmony between the force within you as well as the life force outside of you is shaping what happens in your life. Connecting to the dimension of force you have within to determine your life is the greatest aspect of connecting to the divine in you. There are literature and endless motivational rhetoric about how you determine your life. If you just work hard enough, you can have any type of life you desire; and this is a fraction of the truth. Many variables affect our lives; our health, our personal network, or access to a network that can help us, the community we come, and even mental comprehension. Of course, some people will sure enough tell you, if there's a will, there's a way. I believe in very few absolutes; however, one I don't subscribe to is that every person automatically has an equal playing field to obtain the life they desire.

I believe we are divine, and there is a powerful force within us that can bring amazing realities to pass; however, I know there are equally as great forces outside of us that contribute to our lives as well. I, as an individual, may not be able to control myself being a refugee, or having my village or town blow up my religious radicals or fundamentalist. I may not individually be able to stop my child dying at the hands of a law enforcement officer or being in a car accident. I may not be able to prevent myself from getting laid off. Life is 10% what happens to us and 90% how we respond. Our mindset, our reactions, and our perceived sense of control can cause miraculous occurrences in our lives.

Nurturing the Spirit

The spirit is sensitive to all stimuli, similarly to the mind and body. Being mindful of your emotional experiences, noise, and images can allow you to take whatever necessary steps to honor your spirit. It is in the moments of stillness and internal states of silence and peace that we can connect to our spirits. We nurture the spirit thru acts of restoration, replenishment, and preservation. How you care for and manage your emotions, or attempt to support, hold or manage another's beings' emotions, impact how diminished or full your spirit can be. Ever consider how you can feel fatigued or drained after leaving a large gathering, or completing a conversation with certain people? The energy that you used to engage with the person has depleted you, and your spirit needs replenishment. Have you considered how no matter how much sleep you get from your off days, sometimes you feel completely depleted after work? The nature of your work, or the energy that surrounds you while doing your work, may mentally and spiritually drain you?

Exposure to violence, torture, misfortune, and various forms of oppression, whether in real-time or via media, can absolutely be depleting to the spirit. One can feel worn down as if life can be dually too heavy while you're floating above existence. The phrase, "my spirit is weary," is a prime example of what many individuals feel when they consider not living or wanting to give up on life. Relationships, work, conversations, roles, and responsibilities can all take a toll on our spirits. It's the type of weight that feels light and heavy simultaneously. You can feel so overwhelmed to the point that it feels like you are floating outside of yourself, yet feel overtaken by the weight of life.

Your spirit feeling nurtured is the sensation you experience when you step into or atop a mass piece of land and feel like your breath has been taking away, seeing the world from a high peak like a canyon, major hill, balcony looking over a city, etc. Your spirit is what feels a sense of awe when you are amazed by being in the presence of something greater than you. It's the lightness you feel when you're able to connect to moments of gratitude deeply.

Your spirit is nurtured by anything or anyone that represents love. Love is light. Your spirits' default condition is one of light, peace, love, and guidance. Your spirit guides you. Your spirit reflects the highest state of your existence. If your spirit is compromised by darkness in any way, it's difficult for it to reflect light. When you are constantly around forces of darkness, it impacts your spirit. Darkness is anger, hate, guilt, shame, regret, bitterness, discontent, jealousy, and envy. It impacts your ability to be guided by your spirit. It impacts your ability to trust yourself. It impacts your ability to operate inflow. It impacts your ability even to feel gratitude.

Nurturing your spirit takes effort to be in spaces or around people that fill you up; pour into you. It means doing activities that allow you to tap into a place of pure consciousness. Doing activities that even make you feel the pure joy a child does. Being around people who get you; who see you. To be seen, to be truly seen, beyond the masks, beyond the roles, beyond the images, beyond the facades, is validating. It's the experience one has when you can look at another, and they know exactly what you're thinking or feeling, without any words. See, we can connect beyond the five senses. When someone sees you, it's as if they completely see you beyond anything that the senses can comprehend. You feel each other's kinetic connection. They say something and your spirit reacts because it's as if they used your voice. When they speak, your spirit feels a sense of comfort.

Nurturing of the spirit can surely occur with elements and in stillness. The elements, such as earth, wind, water, and fire, are all representations of the spirit. It is in nature that we re-connect to ourselves. To truly be enlightened about our presence, it's important always to remember, energy can never "die." It constantly moves from one form to another. We often can feel grounded and peaceful in nature because we are experiencing pure energetic connection. Connection is nurturing. Finding stillness within yourself no matter where you are, is the number one way to be connected to yourself, which consequently allows you to nurture yourself. When you are connected to yourself, you know what you need and when you need it. When you are connected to yourself, you can sense the changes in your body. You can gage what your limits of physical engagement look and feel like. Stillness creates an inner state of silence. In silence, you can hear and feel what you typically couldn't if you were in constant motion.

As you move forward in considering the 4th commandment, make sure to ask yourself, *what in my life is nourishing my spirit? What in my life, threatens, poisons, or starves my spirit?* Be as intentional as you can. Move accordingly. Choose accordingly. Your spirit is the essence of you; therefore, nurturing your spirit is really about nurturing the core and essence of who you are.

Commandment 5: Forgiveness

Choosing to Let Go

The only emotion more powerful than forgiveness is love. Yet, they are so connected because, in order for one to forgive, they must connect to the power of love. Love is the only medicine to heal a broken heart or spirit. It is in love that we choose to accept what we've done to someone or ourself; it is in love that we choose to accept what we've allowed someone to do to us or what someone felt that they had the right to do to us. This is why forgiveness is the last commandment of self-love because it takes a massive amount of love to forgive. Love is not something that just overflows non-stop. It is a state that we choose to share but must feel filled up with, in order to give. When we can have love for ourselves, in other words, learn to accept ourselves, it is then that we can pay forward that acceptance and extend it towards someone else.

The act of forgiveness is never for someone else. Oh no! The act of forgiveness is always for ourselves.

Unforgiveness creates an emotional prison. It's a prison that blocks us from shining our best, loving our best, living our best, and opening to others. Unforgiveness is like a dark cloud over the possibilities of our life. When we harbor unforgiveness, it doesn't affect anyone else as much as it affects us. Unforgiveness is like a poison. It will infiltrate different parts of your psyche without you even realizing it. One of the very many reasons I love the art and science of acupuncture, is that you get to learn about the mind-body connection. You get to learn how much impact our emotions have on our physical health.

What does forgiveness mean? In my conceptualization, it means to understand, accept, and let go. It is not a means of excusing a behavior or making a declaration that one's behavior is to be allowed. It's a path of practicing awareness, accountability, empathy, compassion, caution, and assessment.

In practicing forgiveness towards the self, there is a very strong emotional experience, which in and of itself is a heavy reason to let go of what one is holding on to. Shame – When activated, shame is tied to worry, anxiety, fear, and intense feelings of stress. Shame pushes us to lie or not be completely honest. Shame pushes us to hide and isolate. It pushes us to harm ourselves, and walk away from a life we believe we are not deserving of. For the heaviness of shame alone, learning to forgive is powerful.

Exploring Forgiveness

Moving into forgiveness is not an immediate step or short-term process. Forgiveness is very similar to the grieving process. It takes time, conversations, discomfort, hurt, guts, and, most importantly, the power of letting go. In letting go, you move towards the foundation of self-love, acceptance.

It's not the kind of acceptance that would require you to forget what you've done or what someone else has done to you, but it's the act of acceptance that allows you to be present, and confront that past as its novelty. The biggest challenge that most beings have with forgiveness is the process of acceptance for one's own spiritual atonement. Very few leave this Earthly realm unscathed by the actions of others. That means many, if not most of us, have been hurt by someone, and have hurt someone ourselves. In such conditions, it would seem that we would know the value and importance of forgiveness. Thus, being able to accept that we are beings that hurt and get hurt can support the process of acceptance, if we are choosing to thrive beyond the level of harboring hurt, anger, and bitterness.

With acceptance, you can face someone or a situation head-on. You can acknowledge the role it played on your spiritual, emotional, mental and physical well-being, while also owning up to the fact that you gave into the power of hurt and held onto a narrative that keeps you hostage. Acceptance is not about blaming yourself or anyone else. We are all connected and at will to one another. There are constant revolving factors that impact how or why we're drawn to someone. There are many complexities as to why we engage with the people we choose to. On average, people do not blatantly and overtly request that another person hurt, deceive, or dishonor them in some way. Even when we make decisions, at the moment, we are making judgments based on circumstance and what our mind believes is the best decision at that moment. To not accept what was or what is, as is, is a state of torture. Acceptance does not mean agreement or enjoyment. Being in a state in which a grudge, anger, bitterness, and hurt linger, is a state of spiritual imprisonment.

Well, yea Tiffany, but what if I can still be cordial with the person or I don't outwardly express discontent? My friend, my fellow beautiful being, it does not matter. Because when any fear or its cousins (anger, bitterness, etc.) live in our heart space, we are a prisoner. It's the reason why there could be blockages in our life. Some relationships go well, and others don't. It's the reason why sometimes we can feel satisfied with ourselves and open to others, and then at other times, it seems like such a challenge.

At this moment, I want you to take inventory of your relationships and how you show up in different spaces for different people. Is it consistent? Are you consistently honest and open? Are you consistently non-judgmental? Are you consistently accepting? Are there times when there is an immediate shift in your mood? Are there people who have offended you in the past, but even in your present interaction with them, you are standoffish? If you answered yes, after your honest assessment, then the cause for any of these incidences is because of your restless spirit.

Consider a prisoner in a jail cell. It is small. It is limiting. It is solitary. As a result of the conditions a prisoner must face in their domain, they are often restless. In need of stimulation, they seek to exercise, read, yell, or interact with other prisoners, or find a way to express their aggression. They are restless. Similarly, to an inmate that has not come to terms with the confinement of their physical location, your soul can not be at peace because of your conscious or subconscious decision to confine the love that can exist within you. You have confined, imprisoned and compartmentalized your love.

Let's take a common example of childhood trauma. I say common not to minimize the impact of experiencing a childhood that involved abuse or neglect from caregivers but to provide a backdrop for very related experience. Let's say that you had a parent that was emotionally and physically unavailable and who verbally abused you. They were emotionally unavailable because vulnerability was something they were either uncomfortable with or felt like they couldn't access. They were physically unavailable due to being gone often. Their absence could have been due to work, traveling, institutionalization, physical illness, or mental illness. Verbal abuse is characterized by the use of language to hurt, demean, belittle or control another. One can hide or conceal thoughts, information or feelings. One can be argumentative, aggressive and/or confrontational. One can discount another's feelings by name-calling, minimizing their feelings, or deny their feelings as valid.

Verbal abuse can often happen in parent-child relationships due to the dynamic of power that comes with age and hierarchy. Passed down ideas of fear and toxic driven respect are also culprits.

Indeed, forgiving an abusive parent is complicated. Especially when you get to a place of awareness of the severity and impact of the cycles of abuse or neglect you were caught in. Sometimes abuse and neglect is covert, and understanding how even the most covert actions have had an impact you, warrant your forgiveness. For example, let's say anytime you completed a task or put forth effort to accomplish something, this parent often exclaimed that you could do better, or that greatness was expected, so there's no need to receive accolade. When you didn't perform well this parent would come down on you and express how your failure to excel would lead you down a road of failure, and you would never become an adult of accolade. As a child you worked very hard to get the approval of this parent. As you got older, your esteem diminished, and you worked overtime to become an overachiever. You obtained success and accolades, but nothing is ever enough because you are always striving to obtain the approval of that parent. At some point in your adulthood, your parent realizes they were wrong and begins to affirm you and all your life's accomplishment. Because you are so stained with hurt, critique, and judgment, it's hard to accept their new-found love, and you still don't even like being around them.

This is what unforgiveness looks like — being driven by hurt while also letting it affect your being in how you show up. The inability to forgive can allow you to harbor unprocessed emotions and impact your communication or expression of emotions. Your harboring may cause you to become passive-aggressive, completely shut down passively, or express yourself thru the extreme. From time to time, you make snarky comments about your parents and even challenge the authenticity of their words. You don't trust them and rather stay away from them because you carry the narrative that "they've always been negative."

All this goes to say; it's not as if there aren't people that uphold patterns of being unsupportive, unkind, and unhealthy that would serve you to stay away from. What is important is that you understand the importance of not hanging onto the actions of others to the point that it disrupts your sense of peace, or connection to yourself. If you see thru reflection that you've chosen not to release the pain of the past and you see some issues are impacting your wellness, ask yourself, is it actually the spirit of imprisonment that is impacting your inability to thrive fully? Is it the lingering pain or the deep sore of abuse that has prevented you from being open and have you resisting the acceptance of this love in the present? Even if in the present this parent (or any person) continues to make offenses, could you with an open mind and open heart, accept them, and let go of the pain that you rather hold on to?

Could you own the fact that as a child, all you wanted was love and adoration, but this parent gave you the opposite, and that hurt child within you continued to walk beside you as you went thru the world and created your own experiences? Could you own the fact that the story your parents told you really had nothing to do with you, but you decided to hold their own narrative against them and the world for that matter? Could you own the fact that as a child you had limited power, but as an adult you had infinite power and still decided to give it away to the hurt and pain you felt as a child? Could you admit that your parents did the best they could, even if it to your standards as an adult it wasn't good enough?

Would you be brave enough to own the fact that you are enough without validation from someone else? Would you be secure enough to solidify your worth without measuring yourself based on the acknowledgment, affection, or affirmation provided by a parent, caregiver, role model, or any other influential person in your life? Would you admit that you need to learn how to step outside of that limiting narrative taken on by your parent, and be your own cheerleader?

I hope you can realize that there is so much power around and within you, and the source of that power will defeat in counter-narrative to your greatness, magic, and magnificence that anyone can propose. The ex, the friend, the stranger, boss, sibling, colleague who said you were not enough; woman enough, sexy enough, attractive enough, intelligent enough, strong enough, good enough, fast enough, or whatever belongs in front of enough is the counter-narrative to the truth. Let that go. Let their narrative go. If you are your own enemy, let it go.

People make their choices, and as an outcome of those choices, we are sometimes affected. That effect leads to hurt, sadness, disappointment, distrust, anger, but why should we be imprisoned because of another's choices when we have an infinite amount of power to rise above those choices and live our life on a frequency grander than our offenders can imagine.

Forgiveness allows you to say, that person's mess has nothing to do with me, and I'm not going to let it stick to my spirit because I know that I am enough, and my spirit deserves to continue to soar.

Addicted to Self-Critique

I believe self-inflicted criticism and judgment is really the kryptonite for those who are pursuing self-love. It was during a reflective moment that I realized that embarking on an intentional self-love journey for myself was something that would be extremely beneficial and necessary. I had recently completed a relationship, and after I realized that I was beating myself up about a series of decisions that I had made in the relationship, I asked myself. Why are you being so hard on yourself? With the accumulation of all this criticism that I inflicted on myself, all the guilt and all the anger that I held within myself about my decisions, I said to myself, Tiffany, why are you not gentler with yourself? If I can be gentle to other people, why can't I be gentle to myself? On the flip side, I also realized the reason that it can be so easy to critique and be critical of other people because criticism was my safe place. I was just as critical to other people as I was to myself.

I believe with so many stimuli showing us how to be obsessed with self-improvement and being the best; it really creates an anxious incubator of self-critique. We are constantly trying to "measure up" to something or some ideal as opposed to us just being our best. So we look for external measurement, even if no one else is putting the pressure on us directly. We then began to look inward and bring out our critical judge to rule us as inferior, incomplete, and not enough.

I believe that people are so addicted to self-critique. They don't even realize they're doing it. They wake up, look in the mirror, and from the beginning of awareness, they dwell on thoughts and say I'm not good enough. There's nothing wrong with taking self-assessment, but to the degree that you are never content with who you are or to the degree that you never accept who you are, it's dangerous. Throughout the day, it's the simple statements that we make to ourselves like oh my hair is not good enough, my face is not attractive, oh I'm in traffic, why didn't I take another direction; I'm at this job that I hate, I hate my life and I can't believe I got to this point; my boss got mad at me, why don't I do better; we look back at a conversation, at a relationship and look back at interactions, and think, why didn't I do or say this better? We may consistently ask ourselves "why," but not from a frame of exploration and understanding, but a point of harshness and judgmental.

Criticism can be challenging to let go of, especially if it feels like a default position. Our ability to critique ourselves is an ability that some take pride in. However, some critique can be dangerous or debilitating even if it's imparted on us by ourselves. I can speak from experience, that critique can be much more comforting and natural than celebration or praise. Critique can blind us from the beauty of ourselves, life, and experiences that we are critiquing. Yes, critique can serve its purpose when it comes to analyzing how improvements can be instituted in our lives; however, the magic word is moderation, moderation in all things, even in self-improvement. It's about balance, or as a good friend of mine would say, harmony.

In forgiveness, we let go of the harboring or grudging judgment attached to our biases and allow it to be what it is. When we inflict constant critique, it's as if we are harboring ill-feeling and a lack of acceptance towards ourselves and our decisions. It's as if we can't accept that what we did was enough. We were enough in a moment, in a season, and in a circumstance.

For me, I realized that my critical voice was responsible for carrying the narrative, "You are not good enough." A consistent, "you can do better, or why didn't you do X, Y,Z," also came to mind; Tiffany, you don't make adequate decisions when you need to. You are not aligned with your higher guidance system. I'd like to speak to my awareness of knowing my rational and irrational self; When I hear and am aware of the latter narrative playing, I let my irrational self know that it could kick rocks because I'm not accepting such lies or a specific time isn't the time to listen to a narrative of deficiency. Even if it's true that I could do better or more next time, next time doesn't matter if I'm in the midst of celebrating and honoring right now.

Acknowledging how much power I previously granted my critical voice was a major breakthrough in my personal self-love journey. It took me time to gain clarity around the root of the voice. I also had to learn what typically allows my critical voice to rise. Lastly, I had to understand what I do to starve or feed the voice.

In understanding the simple complexity of feeding into our self-criticism, I would like to share Native American proverb:

A Cherokee grandfather talks to his grandson about life. "A fight is going on inside me," he says to the boy. "It is a terrible fight, and it is between two wolves. One is evil- he is anger, envy, sorrow, regret, greed, arrogance, self-pity, guilt, resentment, inferiority, lies, false pride, superiority, and ego." He continued. "The other is good- he is joy, peace, love, hope, serenity, humility, kindness, benevolence, empathy, generosity, truth, compassion and faith. The same fight is going on inside of you – and every other person, too."

The grandson thought about it for a minute and then asked his grandfather, "Which wolf will win?" The grandfather simply replied, "The one you feed."

As wisdom reveals, practicing love, acceptance, and forgiveness will starve our egos desire to inflict criticism. The more love, acceptance, and forgiveness we practice, the less we will find the need to critique ourselves.

Parental Pain

So much of the dysfunctional behavior and mindsets that adults operate in are rooted in pain inflicted on them by their parents. Pain can be the result of verbal, emotional, physical abuse or neglect. Whether as young, teenage or adult children, one can experience pain from their parent thru ostracization, disrespect, disloyalty, demeaning, or manipulation. As adults, many individuals do not even realize that part of their motivation to become "someone" is fueled by parental pain. It can be fueled by desire to gain approval from a parent that is often communicating disappointment or to get the attention of a parent that has often emotionally or physically neglected you. There are individuals who have been abandoned by their parents, and such neglect has been motivation for them to say, even if not to the face of a parent, look at me, I am somebody.

Parental pain is the strongest determinant of our sense of security in or lack thereof in the world. Without the healthy security that can be instilled by a parent, we become adults looking for satisfaction in life in order to fill emotional voids when in truth experiences, accolades, money, or materials can ever replace or fill voids. Voids are the representation of the power we have given to someone that has little to no connection with us. Instead of looking for fulfillment in external sources, the way to fill the void is to take back our power by forgiving that parent. When we forgive, we let go of the resistance of darkness that kept us captive and incomplete. When we are filled with light, we feel whole because we are open. We are open for love to flow in and out. We are to allow goodness to flow in out. When we let the darkness consume, it's as if light or love does not know where to dwell. It may puncture our souls, but it doesn't have space just to settle and radiate.

Many adults spend their whole lives looking for others' approval because it represents the opposite of what they experienced with their parents. They are driven by the lack of genuine love and care in their parental-child relationships and are looking to make up for it in any other relationship. Because we typically see our parents as authoritative figures, someone with parental pain could look to the approval of other authoritative figures or even had constant conflict with other authoritative figures.

Authoritative figures can include but aren't limited to teachers/instructors, work superiors, spiritual/religious leaders, law enforcement, landlords, and government officials.. Imagine being in a meeting with your boss, and they do something that triggers you because when you see them or their behavior, what you're really seeing is your painful behavior that your parent engages in. As a result, you have a negative response and create conflict between your boss and you, either resulting in disciplinary action, or you being fired.

The pain from our parents can leave a bitter stain to the point that we are driven to become versions of ourselves that resemble nothing like them. We put pressure on ourselves to be "better" or different than them because we are so hurt by or dissatisfied with their behavior. One of the worst types of pressure to have is that which is self-instituted. Anything that feeds a monster of criticism and criticalness can be dangerous. We can beat ourselves up and view ourselves as unworthy. Our failure to live up to our own standards can be misguided and can be met shorthand at times.

No one's parents are without fault or limitations. If you think your parents are perfect, that means that you actually don't know them very well. When we can choose to forgive someone who is important to us, and represents an idealistic model of love, safety, and protection, we build the foundation of learning to accept and forgive ourselves. Some of our personality is passed down by our parents and incubated in the environments that we dwell in. This means that some of the best of us, and the worst of us, come from our parents.

As you begin to unpack the impact of your parental relationships on your psyche, it is very possible to grow and develop anger, bitterness, confusion, and possibly even distrust. You begin to see your parents in a light that challenges what we know to be true; the shadow of their humanity and imperfection. In no way are we taught to consider that those older than us, carrying titles to be revered and respected, are imperfect. As you are a collection of environmental and genetic factors that have shaped you, so are your parents.

Lover Pain

The experience of being in love can absolutely change your life. When in love life, all the good things in life can be heightened. Depending on the person we are with, we may push ourselves to be better people. We can literally see life from a new set of eyes. Researchers have said that people in relationships can live longer lives. Men with supportive partners tend to have a higher net worth and accomplish more of their goals than if they were single. Being in a healthy relationship can boost confidence and improve self-esteem. The key to the positive impact of love is grounded in being in a healthy relationship.

Healthy relationships, no matter how positive they are, can still not work out and come to completion. When such relationships complete themselves, we experience periods of grief. In grief we may experience sadness, regret, and denial, but at some point we come to terms with transition. For those who are not in completely healthy relationships, where boundaries are not respected, where abuse or neglect in any form may be present, where lack of respect ensues, the scars or lasting pain from the relationship can cause long term impact. The stains of a lover or partner's pain can result in you losing trust for yourself or others. It can result in diminished esteem and the desire to become emotionally numb or unavailable.

Partner pain is not an experience that only has to occur once a relationship is completed. Pain can be experienced while in a relationship as well. Therefore, being able to understand, process and navigate the pain while experiencing it at the moment is just as important.

The first step to take is to ask yourself, why? *Why are you experiencing the pain you're experiencing? Where does it come from? When does it happen? How often does it happen? Under what conditions is it affecting you the most? Are there any patterns of thoughts or emotions that connect your current pain, to a past pain? What does the pain reveal about the person causing it? Most importantly, how responsible do you feel about the pain?*

I once had someone ask me for advice to help them regarding their husband being depressed and over committing himself to help others. She believed he was trying to distract himself from his stress and problems. The wife was not only concerned about her husband, but it seems that she was beginning to tie her value to her inability to help him. She constantly overextended herself emotionally and mentally to try and be the void she thought her husband needed. She overextended herself believing she could "fix" him. It became apparent that she was failing to do the very thing flight attendants teach you in the safety video: put your mask on before helping others. What I ended up realizing in this conversation is how much the wife needed to understand and practice self-love, learn how to take care of herself, and really reflect on her role in her relationship. As she shared conversations with her husband, I realized she constantly mentioned herself. She would say lines like, "I'm trying to help you, but you won't let me in" or "I'm tired and don't know what to do. I'm trying my hardest to be here for you, but you won't let me. I'm your wife, and I'm here to support you. "She kept mentioning how often she would tell her husband to tell her how he felt or how his distance was affecting her. She kept making her husband's actions about her, and in her own way, constantly pleaded with him to see, understand, and validate her, as well as make her feel needed.

She was in pain and didn't even realize it. Her pain was one of abandonment. Her pain was one that challenged her sense of value and purpose. When we see our value thru productivity or our ability to "do something" whether for a cause or for someone, it is typically a sign that we could stand to develop a deeper relationship with ourselves. She became so consumed with wanting to be his savior; she forgot to be her own. Because he wouldn't open up or take heed to the suggestions she provided him, she began to feel defeated and questioned if she was a "good enough wife." In our conversation, we explored how guilty she felt and how that guilt transformed into shame.

We cannot control the experience that someone else around us is having. However, we can contribute to it. Choosing how we contribute is a power that many of us take for granted, yet at the same time, we can put way too much weight on. Out of love and empathy you may truly hurt and feel sorry for the pain or struggle your partner is experiencing. This is normal. This is ok because you are connected. But when you take in their pain and feel like you're responsible for releasing them from that pain, you must honor and forgive yourself. On the other end of the spectrum, if in a relationship, someone is engaging in behaviors that hurt us like lying, cheating, or ignoring us, assuming that we are deserving of such behaviors because of self-imposed judgments, is also self-deprecating.

Forgiveness doesn't have to be limited to actions that you imparted on someone. Sometimes, it's about releasing emotional ties and expectations that you've imparted on yourself on behalf of your own judgment. When you feel responsible for someone you think and say things like, "I could do more, they feel this way because I'm not doing something, I'm not good enough to help/save them, if I were the right mate, they wouldn't feel this way." Unless you are creating an unhealthy atmosphere for your relationship with aggression, arguments, disloyalty, verbal, emotional, or physical abuse, understand your partner's pain has less to do with you and more to do with them. Relationships can be complicated. Romantic relationships can be complicated. People are complicated. There's a balance to understanding what you do and don't have control over or an impact on. s

When it comes to being in a relationship, there are gaps in communication, sensitivity, and even commitment that people experience when entering in a relationship. There's a balance to understanding how much of the gap can be improved by personal development, therapy tools, or organic growth. One must also know when there are major challenges, which show up as threats to your wellness and connection to self, so be mindful of what you allow, tolerate, or accept. If your partner is stressed and they don't want to disclose what's going on with them, that's ok. If your partner is depressed and won't seem to open up or warm up to your gestures, that's ok. If your partner just experienced a major life transition and they're trying to wrap their head around it (job loss, loss of a loved one, a debilitating event, etc.), that's ok. The challenge is understanding how these events and

231

behaviors can grow into patterns of abuse, neglect or emotional disconnection in the relationship, resulting in pain.

The pain that comes as a result of a romantic connection, like the pain from a parent, can completely uproot and dishevel one's sense of self. Processing the pain, and learning to release it, is so important to your self-love journey. If it's possible to learn from the pain, as opposed to letting it imprison you and prevent you from living your life, make your best effort to do so. Remember, that no one leaves this Earthly experience unscathed. If we can find understanding and gain insight from the pain, we can continue to evolve. Be mindful of letting the pain from a lover/partner rob you of hope, optimism, or trust. Be mindful of the pain allowing fear to encroach in your heart space.

Regardless of the pain you experience, you are loveable. You are deserving of love. If you've experienced someone disregarding you, disrespecting you, ignoring you, belittling, or not attending to you, you are worthy of nurture, support, gentleness, and acknowledgment. On your journey, if you can remember who you are, it can also empower you to forgive someone because of the limits they possess, while knowing you deserve more.

Disappointment From Every Direction

I believe hurt, and all its relatives have a greater effect on us. Hurt can compound, and when it does, it leads to bitterness, the inability to trust, insecurity, fear, doubt, and for many people, hopelessness. In the book "The Compounding Effect," by Darren Hardy, the author suggests that life is not the consequence of major decisions but small decisions. Those decisions can shape your life. Little, everyday decisions will either lead you towards the life you desire or towards life filled with lots of disasters. Such an idea can also be applied to how we process and deal with emotional experiences that we register as hurt, or deeper, disappointment.

Disappointment can foster hopelessness, doubt, and pessimism. Experiencing many disappointments over a lifetime can create a dismal outlook on what possibility looks like. It's as if your light of hope was completely obliterated with darkness. Hearing someone say that they are disappointed in you seems to have a deeper impact than someone preaching to you about your behavior, yelling, or exclaiming their anger. If you're someone who grew up used to verbal or emotional abuse, you can even develop a shield for criticism and overt aggressive behaviors; it's something you could shrug off. However, if there was just an intense stare, a calm tone, followed by the words," I'm just disappointed," it may have a deeper impact on one's sense of self. When someone tells you they are disappointed in you, or if you feel that someone who respects or loves you a lot says they're disappointed, it's almost as if you can equate it to being a failure. There's something about the word disappointment that resonates at another level.

Understandably so, when we get to the point where we are the ones who feel disappointed with others, it almost feels like our hope, belief or trust in someone has been mistreated, or depleted. Sometimes the experience of disappointment can leave us feeling emotionally numb to whoever caused it. We see them differently. We treat them differently. We don't put the same faith in them. We can be so removed emotionally that our mind somewhat blocks out or recategorizes that person's role or importance in our lives. Experiencing disappointment brings forth a reason to work on forgiveness.

Let's pose the question, *what is the root of this disappointment?* I can assure you that most of the time, it stems from you living from a place of expectation and judgment. Disappointment can also come not believing that we or the reflections of ourselves are not good enough. Your disappointment is a type of unforgiveness. As beings embracing our self-love journey, we must consider how we can take disappointment and translate it to acceptance. When we live from a space of expectation, we open ourselves up to the experience of expectation. When we have no expectations, nothing can sneak up on us and surprise, shock, or disappoint us. Think about it. *What would happen if you released expectations and decided to embrace standards and intentions as a foundation for your relationships and life experiences?* Standards create a desired minimum, whereas expectations feed into a controlled ideal, ideals that are created in our head and heart about what SHOULD happen in OUR world. Contrary to what governs your expectations; in reality, people are not in your world; they are mere passers-by. They flow in and out of your world, but they live on their own.

We want to control what other people do or what we believe they SHOULD do based on our biases. When in comparison, standards allow us to express what is acceptable in our life. Standards outline how someone treats us, but it does not dictate who someone is. Expectations put guards, rulings, and frames around someone else's individuality, which at the end of the day, is up to them, not us.

Letting It Go and Confronting Truth

Forgiveness isn't just about verbally affirming to yourself or someone else that you have processed an experience and are now letting it go. There's another aspect of forgiveness to take into consideration. It's also about the art of confronting the truth in order to let go of any sorrow, guilt, shame, or disappointment attached to it. You must acknowledge for yourself that an event has impacted you. You must explore why the event had the impact it had on you, and why the specific emotions that you are experiencing are coming up. Confronting the truth about an experience could and often is more uncomfortable than the act of saying you forgive someone. Admitting that you feel how you feel because of action can be difficult for someone, as discussing, admitting or confronting certain emotions is really uncomfortable. Why is it that confronting the truth can be so uncomfortable?

Well, the truth in itself can be a very uncomfortable notion. Truth implies accountability, and due to the sensitivity of our egos, it's frequently a very difficult task for most individuals to accept. Truth involves vulnerability. At the same time, the truth can be subjective. There is no ownership in accepting that you are a part of a group that has experienced historical oppression; however, you can decide that the injustices and misunderstandings that exist, will not take away the power in your purpose to create opportunities that impact others. There is a sense of ownership in admitting that you feel unseen, unimportant or not enough because of the actions of others or institutions. Admitting that the feeling of deficiency has created anger, and difficulty in forgiveness, is the key. Of course, confrontation, truth revelations, and forgiveness are not just about others; it really is important to also focus on the process to forgive yourself.

Consider this: Is it easy for you to apologize to anyone you offended or hurt? Even if you don't believe like you were in the wrong? If the answer is no, then you understand why accountability is a tough concept for most. When you confront the truth, you are also possibly confronting a series of related events, actions, and experiences that were /are connected to the seedling of truth in need of confrontation.

I recall the moment I confronted an uncomfortable truth shaped by an extended history of trauma: I had a fear of men. It was uncomfortable because I had to dig deep and reflect on the root of that fear. Now this fear wasn't with all men and all settings. It was about being in intimate spaces with men; whether it was close, quiet, and one on one or even just being in a romantic relationship.

Owning the truth was a gateway that caused traumatic and hurtful memories to come to surface, in exploration of this truth I made the decision to not only verbally confront how much these experiences affected and shaped my fear, but I actually confronted the sources, which happened to be specific men in my life who I feel like compromised my security and safety of being with men. I could have continued to suppress these feelings. I could have ignored them. I could have talked myself out of believing that certain people and situations had an impact on me. However, I decided to bring the truth to the light and face it.

It was extremely uncomfortable because, in the process of confronting the truth, I had to own all the actions that I took as a result of my fear. It was a cycle that had occurred over the years. Individuals hurt me, I hurt myself, and I hurt people along the way. It was an experience of emotions, of overwhelming discomfort, of proud advocacy, and unexpected freedom.

Stepping in truth allows you to wear a badge of honor that says I am surely human; I am surely imperfect; I have been hurt and surely have hurt others or made decisions that, in hindsight could have been better. Many people walk around with masks. The mask that we're most proud to wear is the one that projects the story: Everything is ok.

Now of course, it's great to be in a place where everything is ok, but the reality is, if most people dug deep enough, really asked themselves tough questions and really examined the habits and thought patterns they have, they'd realize what would be maladaptive and not conducive to them living their best life. The decision to step into your truth, genuinely and truly let go of limiting narratives you've told yourself, or have believed from the influences of others, is an act of forgiveness. To let go, to release an emotion or energy that's not loving, is forgiveness.

How would you know if you have successfully let go of a situation or circumstance?

When there is little to no negative reaction, that subject or a stimulus that would remind you of the circumstance presents itself; whether implicitly or explicitly. It's important to know that even though your brain is developed at 25, it continues to make neuron connections into old age. Therefore, as sometimes troubling situations occur in your life, your brain stores the memories and as the memories store, an emotional association will occur. Focus on the importance of letting go. Focus on the freedom of not allowing anything to weigh your emotional freedom down. Harboring anything that allows you not to forgive yourself or another takes a toll on your mind, body, and spirit.

Embarking on the Journey

Boundary Practice & Acknowledging Dysfunction

With all the tools and awareness gathered from being able to delve into the dimensions of self-love, I hope that you have been able to start envisioning your life differently. With self-love being a source of groundedness and who you are, after some time, you will begin to feel a renewed sense of freedom. *What does it mean to be able to be free? To live freely, love freely or be yourself freely?* Freedom goes beyond a philosophical framework. Freedom can be as simple as feeling completely safe in whatever state of life you're operating in. Imagine being able to walk around with no self-consciousness about how others view you; imagine being able to conduct yourself in a professional setting and being completely comfortable with your sense of knowledge and capabilities. Imagine being able to operate in your relationships from a stance of openness. You get to be yourself without judgment or being unconditionally protected from being affected by the judgment. Imagine that you constantly see yourself as the best thing since sliced bread.

Self-love is the key to living a life worth living because it leads you to live a life of freedom. It is one thing to be oppressed and controlled by a system, but to experience self-imposed oppression is the most gruesome type of imprisonment. It has been said of refugees and individuals who've served life imprisonment sentences (even in solitary confinement) that the strength and power of their mind was the driving factor of whether they experienced life feel in free or imprisoned, even if they were physically detained. If we work on our internal states, our external world will begin to resemble our internal world.

In moving forward, as you strengthen your ability to set boundaries, honor yourself , and engage in a forgiveness practice, note the shifts that will occur internally. You walking into and living a life of self -love will not always be aligned with the outside world. Some people will have trouble accepting your new truth and lifestyle. Some people will project their insecurities on you. Some people will regard your transformation as powerful, inspiring, and positive. Others may regard it as harsh, off-putting, and negative. People will be uncomfortable in the way that you take a stand for yourself, and as they do so, you can choose whether or not you want to educate them as to the reason you're living your truth and not the one they want you to live. You don't need or require anyone's permission to grow. The greatest discomfort may come once you start using the word "no" or let a loved one know that you are intentionally setting a boundary and desire for them to respect it. Understand, people respond in confusion and dismay when limits are imposed on them.

The Journey & Friends

Friends are the family we choose in a matter of convenience, similarity, or close proximity. We gather friends in different seasons of our lives and during different points of our self-development. Every friend we pick up in life knows a different part of our personality and life functioning. When we have developed and kept friends from childhood, they collect experiences from childhood to adulthood to reference. Friends during middle or high school know us as we are trying to determine our personal identity and values. Those we meet in our 20s, learn who we are as we transition from dependent to independents. 30s and 40s meet us as we're either ironing out our place in the world or getting settled into the life we've begun to build for ourselves. So forth and so on.

No matter at what point a friend comes in your life, it is important that while you come to terms with what you need and what matters to you on while on your self-love journey, you share it with your friends. Those who interact most frequently with us would benefit from and can better support us if they know what type of journey we're on.

It's important to understand that our self-love journey impacts all of our relationships, especially our friendships. When we get to the point of realizing that what we may have learned, may not serve us for the life we consciously choose to live, we end up spending our adulthood actually un-learning so much of the information that we've been conditioned to know. At any point of awakening or consciousness, we will begin to peel back the layers of our previous truths. Each level of truth, perspective, or understanding that we previously held accommodated space for a specific mindset, for a specific set of behaviors, and for varied tolerance or allowance of certain types of relationships. As we pull back these layers and we renew our minds, we renew our beliefs, we renew our truths, and we renew how we form and maintain relationships.

With each level of enlightenment you step into, your boundaries may shift. The values that matter in your relationships may shift. The needs you have identified for the betterment of your well-being may shift. In all of this movement, inevitably, some relationships will naturally come to completion, while others may have to be proactive in walking away from. I use the phrase come to completion because I believe people, like circumstances, can serve a purpose and offer more understanding to our life experience. If a lesson or chapter has served its purpose, it has completed its function, and the energy from it has transformed into something bigger. Using phrasing such as "the relationship ended" puts more focus on the relationship itself, and creates an unrealistic idea that relationships are a terminal experience. We may no longer interact with someone; however, the memories, the impact, and the experiences shape us and stay with us forever, so there is no "end."

It is also inevitable that people who were used to you being one way will not be able to adjust their minds to accept who you are growing into. There are people that you will collect throughout your life who are ok and understanding of your changes while they remain the same. Some people are uncomfortable with change. Some are resistance to others' changing around them because it puts a mirror up to them that leads them to consider who they are and if there is room for transformation. When you have these types of people who have fixed mindsets, as opposed to growth mindsets in your life, they will unconsciously try to put limits on you.

Because you've done the work necessary to grow into whoever you are and are becoming; you have the tools to assert what you believe to be self-serving for you. When it comes to maintaining, outgrowing, or acquiring relationships, we must always consider the question; *how is this relationship serving me?* Other questions to ask yourself: *How can I show up in this relationship? What does it feel that this person validates or invalidates within me? How are my emotional and mental needs being met? What type of value does this relationship add to my life? What is realistic for me to set as a standard for this relationship? How do I communicate what I will and will not accept in my relationships? How do I give love & receive love?*

How you define friends and friendship is up to you. My suggestion would be to make sure that you understand the role and purpose that people around you have in your life. When you are clear what these roles look like, make efforts to have open and honest conversations to those closest to you, to discuss with each other what these relationships look like.

It's important that we don't keep people in boxes and place them on platforms that make the supernatural and incapable of mistakes. The danger of you creating a box for who they are is that they can step outside of that box anytime they choose, and you may or may not be satisfied with the consequence. The box you framed them in, could be a positive one to you; a box that makes them "good," worthy, loveable, etc. They can change, step outside of your box, into now a negative box, and you experience disappointment, shock, anger, hurt, etc. Alternatively, you could put them in a box associated with negative ideas, and they can step outside of it and do something positive.

This is why self-love is not just about your ability to accept yourself. It is also about your capacity to understand what it takes to accept others and what it takes for others to accept you. Self-love can be lived thru a lens of intentionality. Due to you making choices that allow you to honor yourself, you can be intentional about relationships you nurture, complete, or begin. You can choose what people you allow to be in your life, to support you, be around you. Likewise, you can choose what type of behaviors and relationships you won't keep around in your life. You choose what is acceptable in your life. There are no excuses. If after much assessment, you deep down intuitively, in your gut, know that a relationship is not serving you, regardless of the time you're in relationship with the person, regardless of the effort put into the relationship, regardless of the issues that you and another person have overcome together, if at any point you realize it's not serving you, you have the choice to let it go.

So what does your self-love journey interacting with your friendships look like? It looks like you saying no when you really don't want to say no. It looks like you being comfortable with your decision because they serve you. It looks like being able to make decisions and not being meant to feel guilty or feeling the need to over-explain why you made a decision, to make your friends feel more comfortable. It looks like you knowing and believing that decisions that you make are beneficial for you and understanding that you don't need the insight of those who you consider friends, but should you ask their opinions or insight, it's extra. It looks like you're growing into accepting yourself and your friends being equally, or even more accepting of you as well. It looks like equitable and harmonious relationships. Self-love will constantly challenge you to work on honoring yourself, honoring your mind, honoring your spirit, and practicing forgiveness. If you have friendships that do not allow you to practice these commandments, then you need to assess whether you must have those relationships.

Relationships falter with discontent, bitterness, envy, jealousy, and anger at the core of them. These are often emotional experiences that arise when one doesn't have the space to be themselves, and the relationship threatens their ability to reach self-actualization. If you are in friendship with someone who often harbors these negative emotions or experiences, maybe it's time for them to embark on their self-love journey. At the end of the day, one must ask, is compromising your own peace for the sake of another person's comfort with unhealthy, dysfunctional, damaging, un-nurturing, or toxic behaviors, worth it? If your answer is yes, then continue with such relationships. If your answer is no, then you understand the difficulty, maturity, wisdom, and discernment it's going to take to manage your life, protect yourself, pour into yourself and incubate healthy relationships.

Every time we allow someone to disrespect us, every time we allow someone to challenge what we believe is best for us, every time we give up our power to someone else who feels that they deserve to have power over us, every time we allow ourselves to be belittled, we must ask, is this honoring me? Is this reflective of self-love? We give up our opportunities, moments of peace, harmony, and growth so that someone else feels better at times. Ask yourself, *when I look at this relationship that I have, can*

I say to myself that it's reflective of my self-love journey? Would I say that this friendship is indicative of my perceived worth or value? Would I say that this friendship is the epitome of me honoring myself, honoring my mind, honoring my body, honoring my spirit and practicing forgiveness?

The Journey & Family

When you have been raised and adapted to living in dysfunction, how do you develop the tools, awareness, and recognition to practice self-love amid such dysfunction? One of the key vessels of dysfunction that we don't really have too much control over in our life is our families. My question is, how do you practice self-love and honoring yourself if you have a dysfunctional family? Family-based trauma is something that we don't really talk about we are expected and challenged with the task to be around people because they are family; in the presence of people because they are family; talk to or interact with individuals because they are family. We are challenged to let go of what would be considered a healthy boundary because someone is our family. We are expected to put aside our safety, our peace and our groundedness for a dysfunctional being because they share the same blood as us.

The Journey & Lovers

The deeper and the farther along your walk that you get, you become clearer in who you are. You become clear in what you want, and when it comes to what romantic love looks like, in relation to your self-love journey, you will choose your partners differently. You will attract different partners because you've been able to develop a sense of wholeness within yourself. You operate at a much higher and elevated level in love. Behaviors and scenarios that may have bothered you before or may have been triggered for you, maybe even some standards or ideals that you had in the past, may not necessarily stay with you as you embark on your journey. You're going to become more insightful about yourself. As you become more insightful about yourself, you become more insightful about people.

Some love from a place of brokenness, incompletion, or the belief in self-inferiority. To love like this is to love from a place of void. When you have voids in you, you're looking for other people to complete you. You're looking for other people to make you feel whole; you're looking for someone else to make you feel good about yourself; make you feel worthy or valuable. You're looking for someone to make you feel good enough. When you've begun embarking on and living thru the consciousness of your self-love journey, you learn that the source of inspiration and empowerment and joy and upliftment first begins with you. Of course, our partners can complement our centeredness and add so much more to the beautiful truths we know about ourselves. However, at the beginning and end of the day, how we love, begins with us. It begins with our perception. It begins with our assessment of our value and worth.

I want to paint a picture of how romantic love looks before and after us operating from a consciousness of self-love. Before operating in the consciousness of self-love, we look to our partners to assess who we are, our value, our worth, and what we "should " be doing. Once we are operating in the consciousness of self-love, if our partners provide any type of criticism or critique, what we do is take our time to assess the source of what they're saying. We consider first, if what they're saying is a pure projection of their own experience/reality or if it is aligned with some area of ourselves that can be improved. As opposed to before, what we DON'T do is automatically take the words, absorb them and criticize ourselves. Just because our partner said something negative or critical or just because someone speaks something of you, it does not make it true.

When you don't operate in the consciousness of self-love, you are not fully aware and accepting of who you are. In many ways, you don't really know who you are, so you look to other people, like your partner, to tell you who you are. Once you operate in the consciousness of self-love, you have begun to spend time with yourself, to get to know yourself, to pull back the layers, to be able to accept and acknowledge who you are and in every step of your journey, you know how to honor who you are. Before operating in the consciousness of self-love, we have a limited concept of what it really means to accept and honor our selves. We may know in general what it means to respect ourselves, but frequently our ideals of respect are based upon unreliable models of love that we observed, as well as dependent on the expectations that ourselves and our partners have come to terms and agreement with.

When you're involved in a relationship pre-conscious of self-love, how you and your partner decide to affirm or criticize, support, or tear down one another can be faulty. It can be unproductive. It can be maladaptive, and it can be unhealthy. You may not have been able to understand, comprehend or even be aware of appropriate and necessary boundaries to set with your partner. You may not have set expectations around how you want a partner to speak to you; how you want a partner to treat you. You may not even have been able to communicate what your partner can do to contribute to the self-care tool kit thru their supportive behavior. So what happens is our partners tear us down, often unintentionally, and when they tear us down and breaks our heart, it makes us feel less than and not worthy of love. It makes us so thirsty and hungry to get the approval and appraise from our partners that we then decide to dishonor ourselves, just to be able to satisfy our partners. If we don't live up to their standards and approval, we feel bad, and it's only because we don't even know what our standard of living is. Pre-consciousness of self-love, we are often naïve when it comes to being able to honor our mind, our bodies, our spirits, our selves or what it means to consistently be in a place of practicing self-forgiveness and forgiveness of others while being in a romantic relationship.

This is why operating in the consciousness of self-love brings about a very different relationship. When I'm operating in self-love while in a relationship, I can share my boundaries, I can share what I know my mind, body, and spirit needs to thrive. I can transparently and vulnerably express who I know I am in my totality and present that to a person in a way that lets them know; hey I accept my imperfections, do you? If you can effectively express who you are, from a place of elevated self-awareness and acceptance, you show them how you can be loved. Presenting your best and worst hand upfront allows you to ask, do you accept me? Flaws and all? Because you have done the work and learned how to follow the commandments, you can then help guide your lover. This is how you love me. This is how you accept me. This is how you work with me to help me grow. When those imperfections arise in a relationship where at least one or both parties are not operating in consciousness about self-love, you give your partner the power to be judgmental and critical. That judgment and criticism eventually breaks you down to the point where even if you decided to conclude the relationship, you carry this baggage of worthlessness and helplessness around with you, expecting someone else in the future to pick it up and pull out the contents in order to help and save you; and fill that void.

The Journey & Work

As you embark on your journey, you will awaken parts of you that have been sleeping; parts of you have that have tolerated behaviors and environments that don't serve you, and parts of you that need different environments to thrive. As a result, even your work is affected. If you were previously driven by material success, then you going after a well-paid and highly comparable job is benefitting. However, once you are awakened, and take assessment of not only what you want to do, but also what you're passionate about and possibly what is aligned with your purpose.

When we are speaking of work, I must be honest in saying that I speak from a US citizen who has lived in the US all my life, however, who has traveled abroad.

When it comes to your journey, it's all about the questions you ask yourself — constant questions about how your relationships, your environments, and your actions honor you. You want to ask, *how does this serve me? Is what I'm doing or thinking, allowing me to honor myself?* Such questions allow us to keep ourselves in check; when it comes to our life experiences. So when we look at the intersection between our self-love journey and work, it becomes simple. It comes back to the question; does my job, does my career, does my duties, do these environments, does my relationship with my coworkers, does my relationship with my boss reflect self-love? How you choose your path to income is up to you; some people follow money; some people follow passion and some people follow skill. Some people have been able to manifest the intersection between all three. What makes you initially choose to do what you do is often influenced by your family ideas around success, maybe just the fact that you need to get by and manage your bills in your financials or maybe just the fact that you just need money to provide for your family. We may go after careers that some of the favorite people in our lives have pursued. Sometimes we go after careers because we feel like those are the only attainable options. Sometimes we go after careers because we just end up falling into them by life circumstances. Sometimes our careers are decided for us because of family legacy.

Regardless of what got you in two. No matter where you are or how you got to the place that you're in when it comes to your job or your career, understand that self-love has a place with you in that intersection as well. *What does self-love look like when it comes to your work?* Just like in our relationships and other dimensions of our life at work, self-love looks like boundaries. Self-love looks like respect. Self-love looks like you honoring your time. Self-love looks like you making sure that you give yourself the nutrients that you need to be productive. Self-love looks like you accepting your faults but also celebrating your wins and congratulating yourself for everything that you do. Self-love looks like you taking advantage of your sick leave and your vacation time. Self-love looks like you not being sedentary every day, all day, while you're working. It looks like you standing up in your cubicle space or your office and making sure that you have blood flowing. Self-love looks like you stepping outside of the office, taking a walk, or being in nature. In reference to your work, self-love also means asking yourself the question, *does what I'm doing speak to my self-love journey? Is my job a reflection of my self-love?* This is less about joy and more about the importance flow and alignment. There are days when we feel strong, and there are days when we want to retreat. There are days when we would do our best, and our best looks like a ten and other days our best look like a three. Our work is connected to who we are, therefore at times, whatever is going on in our personal lives we take into work. It is an unrealistic expectation that you will like and enjoy every aspect of your job. However, if you have check ins with yourself about whether your job is honoring who you are and mirroring self-love, and you come to answer no, then it is time to accept where you are and make the decision to either stay or move in alignment with something that serves you for a higher purpose or in a higher frequency.

When you look at yourself in the mirror and ask yourself, does my job reflect what I believe self-love to be? Remember that it is only you that can answer the question. It would not serve you to rely on the perspective of someone else because they are not you. Any person outside of you can give you their perspective, but at the end of the day, you must accept who you are, and you must accept your standard of living, and you must accept what makes you feel aligned and grounded.

Can you connect to a grander or greater purpose when it comes to what you do? Do you feel that if you had to rank your overall satisfaction and your work that you could answer the question that yes, this is a reflection of self-love? If you had to create a check-off list of overall satisfaction of your job and let's say you listed the following categories overall job satisfaction, employee and peer relationships, management relationship, compensation, time management or flexibility, ability to thrive, and ability to take care of oneself. If you had to use a Likert scale, I'd like you to scale to write these things how would they go because it's totally possible that one area could be lacking, but the other would be stronger

Here are some additional questions to raise. *How does this job feed into my perception of myself? Does it allow me to see my best self as well as the self that I know needs improvement? Does this job allow me to honor my mind? Am I being mentally challenged? Am I being mentally stimulated? Am I receiving input and content that helps me grow into my better self? Am I around or in an environment or industry that feeds me what I need in order to get to whateverr my next level is mentally, spiritually, or physically? Does my job honor my body or allow me to honor my body? Am I able to maintain a healthy balanced diet while working my job? Am I able to stay active while having this job or being at my job? Do I find any negative effects of my job on my body? Does my job allow me to honor my spirit? Does my job speak to my purpose? Does my job speak or help me feel like I am in a state of flow? Are there aspects of my job that teach me about forgiveness? Are there aspects of my job that teach me about the power of letting go and releasing what does not serve me?*

Consider your intentions in living. When you compromise in one dimension of your being, it will likely affect or spill over into other dimensions of your being. If you are deciding to live with an intention of self-love, asking honest questions, listening for honest answers, and taking the necessary steps to align yourself with your intention accordingly, is what's important for you. We don't reach our highest potential, make the greatest impact, or establish the best legacies because of doing what others tell us to do.

Constant Growth in Motion

You may never feel like you've arrived, and that is a humble disposition to be in. Even if you've entered a season in your life that you feel extremely comfortable in, it's only a matter of time before life will present you an opportunity to once again, delve inward, and re-assess your relationship with yourself. Your self-love journey is exactly that; a journey. It is a journey in which the only final destination comes at the end of life.

There are always outside distractions and influences that shape how we perceive, treat, and honor ourselves. It is these external influences that shape our internal dialogue. Regardless, if we intend to absorb these outside influences, our minds subconsciously take in information from all sources of stimuli, without our awareness.

Every positive or negative interaction or observation affects us. We take direction from our interaction with the world. The basic psychology of reinforcement is that positive reinforcement typically increases a behavior, while negative reinforcement typically decreases a behavior. As you navigate your journey and champion the five commandments, some subconscious limitation, narrative or poison will eventually challenge you under the right circumstances.

No matter what, you keep moving on. Your love is the light, and the world will present darkness. In growing, we must learn to accept the natural flow and duality of our living experiences. Accepting duality does not mean we make excuses or make ourselves susceptible to certain circumstances because "that's life," but by accepting duality, there will be times when we are up, and other times we are down. There will be times in which we move in every area of our lives with confidence and other times where some areas seem easier to manage and navigate than others. There are times in which we feel like we are winning and other times, we feel like we are failing. Duality is about accepting that two opposing events or conditions can co-exists. You can be a generally optimistic person and feel depressed. Your friend can be dependable and toxic. You can be grateful for your job and generally unhappy with it.

Count every season in your life as perfect. Even if it's uncomfortable, it's perfect. It's perfection because you are living in and receiving exactly what you need to elevate you to your next level. The challenge is being aware of the existing internal tools and resources that you already have to get you to the next level. Self-awareness is key. Some people go thru challenges and get lost in them. They grow into a state of helplessness and a mindset of deficit, therefore limiting their ability to tap into their internal resources, or even evaluate the resources they can obtain from their situation to move past their current circumstances. People get lost in tough times. They get lost in the downtimes. They get lost in confusion. They get lost in loss. They get lost in transition. It is understandable because we all have different levels of resilience; however, as humans, we are all resilient. It is our mindsets and sheer will that determines how we tap into and enact that resilience. We must ask, *how can I grow? What can I learn? What can I take away?*

In practicing or incorporating the 5 Commandments of Self-Love, my intention is present points of consideration so that you feel encouraged to connect to intuitive knowledge and continue to build more. Self-love is not black and white. There is no perfectionism in self-love. There have been many times where I threw my hands up and cried in desperation of wanting answers to the question of why or how? And no matter how low I felt, at some point I always had a shift, and came to understand that I had everything I needed or could access what I needed once I moved past focusing on what I wasn't doing, what didn't exist, or what I didn't have.

Setting aside the histories of oppression and systems that limit certain groups from advancing, there is no one born into this world destined for darkness. Yes, taking into consideration that we all start life from different vantage points and various abilities, navigating life can absolutely be "easier" for some rather than others. However, no one person is born deserving of more purpose, goodness, love, and honor than another.

Life is not "fair" for everyone; however, the awareness, knowledge, and self-love that one acquires and taps into, is solely up to every single individual. No one can live your life for you. No one can make you love yourself. No one can control how you navigate relationships with others in your community or the world. We all have choices. Even if respect or adherence to authority is a value of yours, and authoritative figures order or dictate your behavior, it is still a choice for you to abide by such demands.

We cannot control what others do or what happens in the world around us. All we have true power over is ourselves and our efforts of influence over others. It is this power that we must keep in mind while on our journey. She or he who can be aware of, develop, strengthen, and practice internal power is a unique kind of revolutionary. When most people are too afraid to step outside of society's expectations, norms, and ideals, if they are aligned with their journey, one who chooses to honor themselves and keep their heart open to acceptance is an outlier, an outlier that can influence others. An outlier who subtly teach others how to do the same.

Remember that the journey is all about acceptance and being open to growth. We can read and do as much personal work as possible, collecting ancient pearls of wisdom and life truths; however, we as people are complex. And what we know in theory is often much more difficult to practice, not because we don't want to, but because we are creatures of habits. It takes our minds much time to adjust the schemas and heuristics built up over our lifetimes, and create new ways of being. Research says it takes at least 21 days to build a new habit and at least 90days of persistent practice to make a part of your lifestyle. However, even at 90 days, we can easily revert to our old ways, or not hold on to that new way of being past that very point.

Be gentle with yourself while you are on your journey because there will be forces that will work to disregard the work you have put in. They will throw your past in your present and speak limitations into your future. They will challenge to doubt your growth and your capability; however, it's important to remember that if you intentionally do your best as often as possible, you can always choose to practice the 5th commandment of self-love, forgiveness. Let go of being stuck on your imperfections and embrace what it means for your higher self to be challenged by your lower self. We are working to empower, embrace, and evoke our higher selves, while we are acknowledging, accepting, and slowly killing our lower selves.

As you embark on your journey, pay attention to the experiences that become catalysts for your growth. I believe that each of us has chrysalis-like sources to aid in our metamorphosis or transformation. I have found nature, travel, fitness, and water to always be incubators of reflection, insight, and transformation for myself. When I am outside, whether in pure admiration, sitting on the grass, walking thru the woods, or passing a trail on a hike, paying attention to the growth of trees, seeing the presence of animals, and acknowledging how everything in the natural works in balance, at any moment grounds me. Travel reminds me that there is no one way to exist. It humbles and reminds me of the notion, the more you know, the more you realize that you don't know. It teaches me never to lose my childlike curiosity and to stay in a state of exploration because when you search for answers, you learn so much about yourself. Fitness is always a mirror of my current state of resilience and determination. It also teaches me about balance and the importance of accepting the moment and being gentle with myself. I do my best thinking in water. Whether in a pool, shower, bath, or at the beach, there is something about water that is so transformative for me. Water is the basis of what we spent time before birth in, and it's always represented in religions to symbolize rebirth.

For you, an incubator may also be an element or specific activity. No matter what, find what they are, and engage in them, intentionally, often. You will learn, re-learn, and eventually have to walk in the truths that you collect on your journey. I find it more comfortable to come to the truth and choose to walk in it, as opposed to learning it thru trial and error. Either way, a lesson is a lesson. What life does is present to you a lesson, present to you a test, and then unfold your life in a way that proves you either passed or failed the test. If you fail the test, then life will present you with both the lesson and test again. When you find and connect to your transformation incubators, you get to receive an in-depth lesson, along with a study guide. You have the opportunity to really take in your life, and the implications of who you are, the choices you've made, and how such information can lead you to life that continues to elevate, demote or sustain you.

On your journey, you will understand the meaning of being uncomfortable, feel the fear, and do it anyway. There will be times where it will seem so uncomfortable to choose yourself first. This concept of choosing and honoring self is embedded in many of our ancient religious and spiritual practices, but in most of our cultures we were socialized in, we were taught to do for others first. This disables our ability to stand outside of an interaction or situation and completely, objectively, without the experience of a moral dilemma, to consider how our minds, bodies, and spirits are impacted. Choosing others seems to come more naturally than choosing ourselves us, but it isn't necessarily natural; it's just an unconscious choice made due to socialization.

What do I mean by choosing others?

We choose others when we put their comfort before our own. We choose others when we consider their feelings before our own. We choose others when we consider what they think about us. We choose others when we worry and make choices based on how we think others will perceive us. We choose others when we succumb to societal pressures and standards. We honor others, as we slowly allow ourselves to die.

I believe everything should be strived for in harmony and moderation. I understand that values such as family, community, etc. are important, and acting in a way that demonstrates pride, humility, and respect is important in such frameworks; however, we don't have to consider ourselves martyrs.

Ask yourself this: If you're not the one to do it, will the world end? Will the world, community, or family be different? Will that person's life be completely different? If your answer is yes, then do the thing that seems sacrificial and beyond yourself. Because in truth, there will be moments where we must step outside of ourselves and make decisions knowing that they impact others. The issue lies in the way and the frequency in which we do it.

When we consider our interactions with others and how to honor ourselves, we must make decisions and think about the compound effects. Earlier in the book, I spoke on the topic of complex trauma. Complex trauma is the experience of living thru the occurrence of multiple or differing traumas throughout life at a high frequency. Let's say, for example, over ten years, someone experienced a form of abuse, a chronic illness diagnosis, institutionalization, sudden death of a child by gunshot or unexpected illness, and a robbery, that is considered complex. In understanding something with compounding effects, let's say, just one of these events happens to someone. That would be traumatic, however, over the years, the more and more these types of events have occurred in someone's life, may create a person with an extremely bitter, depressed, and bleak outlook on life.

269

The experience of the trauma has compounded and created a grave disposition for that individual.

When we interact with a toxic person on a regular occurrence, we compound the effects of their negativity on our mind, body, and spirit. When we obsess about the expectations of others, we compound the stress of feeling "not good enough," and develop a compromised self-perception and esteem. Therefore, it is important to ask yourself, *is this interaction worth it? Is it important? Is setting this goal to appease others or make myself likable truly necessary?*

In the end, we are faced with two major questions: how did I live my life? And how will others remember me? The balance comes when we can answer both questions in a way that will leave us fairly satisfied with the answers.

There is something so powerful to be able to stand in who you are. The beauty of life's possibilities is that there is always an alternative perspective. There is always a possibility to see ourselves or the world different. If ever there was an opportunity for you to take on another perspective, which presents itself every day, you can choose to. Until then, until you choose to shift who you are or how you think, there is nothing wrong with you taking pride in your present state.

On the journey, there will be tons of battles, tests, and trials. When you realize that you have the potential or the power to walk an enlightened life. You can step out of dysfunction. You can step out of darkness. It feels amazing to uncover depths of your being that you didn't even know was hidden. That is the value, the promise, the beauty of the self-love journey. Yes growth takes work. Yes change takes work. The work will be worth it, so I encourage you to be and stay open.

For myself, there was a pivotal point where I realized that I came back to myself. If I came back to myself, that means who I was, what I needed to do, to see, to realize, to honor within and about myself, and love myself; it was already in me. I was so focused on trying to fix myself that I did not see my light. I was so focused on fixing the darkness that I allowed the darkness to blind me from seeing my own light. I had the perfect aha moment. I was in some flow of reflection, and just like that, my intuitive self experienced a magical moment. I was in one of those, "Who are you?" types of reflections. I said to myself, wait, Tiffany, all I need to do is pull back this lens. I consciously and spiritually pulled back the lens, and I saw my light. I then realized and affirmed to myself, my goodness, my light, has been here all along.

I thought the bitterness of hurt diminished my light. I thought that shame diminished my light. I thought that the treachery and the betrayal diminished my light. I realized that both my light and my darkness are both residing in the same space. It was then that I took my acceptance to another level, and proclaimed that I'm going to embrace it because it's OK. Just focusing on darkness is not how one accepts, honors and forgives themselves. I will make sure I affirm, uplift, and feed the light which I already know exists within me. I will make efforts to caress the darkness but not from a place of victimization or helplessness.

On your self-love journey, you might get closer to yourself, gain a deeper understanding of who you are, and may actually return to your most pure selves. What you really end up doing is coming back to the essence of who you are and who you always have been. At one point of reflection, after years of trying to manifest the love that I wanted for myself, I came to realize that love was already within me and had always existed in me. It was residual effects of life circumstances that created barriers between my highest self and my lower self. As I was learning to accept certain aspects of my being, I realized that earlier in my life those aspects of my being never had been a problem. Actually, learning to embrace my difficulties, my fears, my strength was pivotal event that changes or altered my relationship with myself.

You come back to who you really are. Life can harden us; life can break us; it can separate us from who we really are and then we choose to parade around as someone else, as something else. But sometimes the form that we end up taking because of life's trials is not who we really are, we end up letting life define us, or shape us negatively. Thru self-love, we can embrace and stay in the groundedness of who we really are.

Never stop asking questions. Never stop listening to the answers. Never stop receiving insight. Never stop learning. Never stop growing. Remember that growth, transformation, elevation, and self-love are not about fixing yourself. You are not broken. You don't need to be fixed. You may have voids. You may have wounds. You may have areas of opportunities, but we all do. We all have blind spots. We all have hang-ups. Let no one, including yourself, allow you to feel so imperfect that you believe that you are not deserving of goodness. The commandments can help guide you on a path of remembering exactly when to make sure you are treating yourself like someone deserving of acceptance, honor, and forgiveness.

It is easy for us to take on our life experiences in a way that suspects us to believe we are not deserving of goodness. My friend, to walk in love, you must know that you deserve it. To honor yourself, your mind, your body, and spirit, you must believe that you are worthy of and deserving of honoring yourself. You must believe that your time, health and wellbeing are worth focusing on. No one can convince you of that better than you. For you to live in freedom, you must believe that you deserve not be bound to grudges and guilt. You must know that forgiveness is valuable for your peace of mind. Once you believe in the value of your freedom, it is then that you will pursue a life that allows you to live out that commandment.

The people outside of us only have as much power of influence as we allot to them. No one can have power over us; it is in giving up our freedom and dishonoring ourselves that we grant them power over us. Not only do I want you to know that you have power, I want you to own your power. Knowing that this power is in you, is what propels you to accept yourself and the way that life unfolds. It will unfold in your favor if you choose to see it that way. It will unfold in your favor if you choose to grow and stay inflow. It will unfold in your favor if you choose to take the best with the worst. It will unfold in your favor if you choose to transmit lessons into success.

It will unfold in your favor if you have confidence in the ability to transform and alchemize all that comes across your path. Remember that acceptance golden. Accept all but hold onto nothing. Harness your power and nurture all that honors you. Love yourself, infinitely. Find infinite love within you because self-love is the key to living a life worth living.

Resources

The 4 agreement. Don Miguel Ruiz

The Power of Now. Ekhart Tolle

Seat of the Soul. Gary Zukav.

The Body Keeps the Score.

ACE Study. CDC.

The Top 5 Regrets of Dying. Bonnie Ware

Maslow's Hierarchy of Needs.

Piagets Stages of Development.

Radical Acceptance

Paul Eckman. Theory of Emotions.

The Compounding Effect. Darren Hardy

References

Amaresan, S. (2019, March 19). *HubSpot Blog*. Retrieved from www.hubspot.com: https://blog.hubspot.com/service/conflict-management-styles

Boeree, C. G. (2009). Retrieved from http://webspace.ship.edu/cgboer/limbicsystem.html

John M. Grohol, P. (2019, June 25). *15 Common Cognitive Distortions*. Retrieved from PsychCentral.com: https://psychcentral.com/lib/15-common-cognitive-distortions

M.D., N. B. (2019, June 21). Retrieved from Psychology Today: https://www.psychologytoday.com/us/blog/hide-and-seek/201601/what-are-basic-emotions

Mark Sanders, L. C. (n.d.). *The 8 Characteristics of Healthy Relationships*. Retrieved from https://irp-cdn.multiscreensite.com/38c63840/files/uploaded/The%208%20Characteristics%20Of%20Healthy%20Relationships.pdf

Resources for Parents. (n.d.). Retrieved from Innerchange.com: https://www.innerchange.com/parents-resources/family-roles/

Terry, K. (2019, May 6). Retrieved from www.verywellmind.com: https://www.verywellmind.com/psychology-basics-4157186

Endnotes

[iii]Max Planck Institute for Human Cognitive and Brain Sciences. "Mental training changes brain structure and reduces social stress." ScienceDaily. ScienceDaily, 4 October 2017. <www.sciencedaily.com/releases/2017/10/171004142653.htm>.

[iv] The Big 5

[v] Courtois, Courtney. Complex Trauma, Complex Reactions: Assessment & Treatment, 2004. Educational Publishing Foundation. Psychotherapy: Theory, Research, Practice, Training.

[vi], Brigham Young University. (2017, October 16). Stress might be just as unhealthy as junk food to the digestive system: Study with mice shows stress causes digestive microorganisms to behave similarly to how they act with a high-fat diet. ScienceDaily. Retrieved October 27, 2017, from www.sciencedaily.com/releases/2017/10/171016142449.htm

[vii] The Body Keeps the Score, Van der Kolk, Bessel (2014)/

[viii]https://www.marketresearch.com/Marketdata-Enterprises-Inc-v416/Weight-Loss-Diet-Control-12225125/

[ix]University of New South Wales. (2017, October 3). One hour of exercise a week can prevent depression. ScienceDaily. Retrieved October 27, 2017 from www.sciencedaily.com/releases/2017/10/171003093953.htm

CPSIA information can be obtained
at www.ICGtesting.com
Printed in the USA
BVHW041553020321
R11938600001B/R119386PG600535BVX00029B/7